COMPREHENDING
SUICIDE

BOOKS BY EDWIN S. SHNEIDMAN

Deaths of Man (1973)
Voices of Death (1980)
Definition of Suicide (1985)
The Suicidal Mind (1996)

EDITED BOOKS

Thematic Test Analysis (1950)
Clues to Suicide (1957) with N. L. Farberow
The Cry for Help (1961) with N. L. Farberow
Essays in Self-Destruction (1967)
On the Nature of Suicide (1969)
The Psychology of Suicide (1970, 1994) with N. L. Farberow
    and R. E. Litman
Death and the College Student (1972)
Suicide: Contemporary Developments (1976)
Death: Current Perspectives (1976, 1980, 1984)
*Endeavors in Psychology: Selections From the Personology
    of Henry A. Murray* (1981)
Suicide Thoughts and Reflections, 1960–1980 (1981)
Suicide as Psychache (1993)

COMPREHENDING SUICIDE

Landmarks in 20th-Century Suicidology

EDWIN S. SHNEIDMAN

American Psychological Association
Washington, DC

First Printing March 2001
Second Printing October 2001

Published by
American Psychological Association
750 First Street, NE
Washington, DC 2002

Copies may be ordered from
APA Order Department
P.O. Box 92984
Washington, DC 20090-2984

In the U.K., Europe, Africa, and the Middle East, copies may be ordered from
American Psychological Association
3 Henrietta Street
Covent Garden, London
WC2E 8LU England

Typeset in Goudy and Zapf Book Light by EPS Group Inc., Easton, MD

Printer: Edwards Brothers, Inc., Ann Arbor, MI
Cover Designer: NiDesign, Baltimore, MD
Technical/Production Editor: Catherine Hudson

The opinions and statements published are the responsibility of the authors, and such opinions and statements do not necessarily represent the policies of the APA.

Library of Congress Cataloging-in-Publication Data
Shneidman, Edwin S.
    Comprehending suicide : landmarks in 20th-century suicidology / Edwin Shneidman.—
1st ed.
        p. cm.
    Includes bibliographical references and index.
    ISBN 1-55798-743-2
        1. Suicide.   2. Suicide—Miscellanea.   I. Title.

    RC569 .S3848 2001
    616.85'8445—dc21

                                                                        00-065066

British Library Cataloguing-in-Publication Data
A CIP record is available from the British Library.

Printed in the United States of America

Lucky me. I celebrate my unaccountable good fortune with everyone
who matters—extraordinary parents, children, grandkids,
mentors, colleagues, friends—and at the very top,
a mild Everest of heart, there's Jeanne.

CONTENTS

PREFACE

This book aspires to be a once-in-a-library source for those interested in the enigma of suicide. The title is meant to imply that no thoughtful reader ought to come away from a serious perusal of this book without a substantial increase in the comprehension of what suicide is, and, by extention, how suicides might be prevented. The core of the book—beyond that of the many how-to-prevent-it volumes that currently flood the marketplace—is a serious effort to examine 13, a baker's dozen, other books representing a panoply of thought on suicide, to read them in their original words, and to contemplate them, albeit briefly, in an essay that puts a new face on an old friend. My injunction to the reader might be, Read them and reap. I mean, of course, reap new thoughts, fresh insights, and unusual and useful understandings and intuitions about the vast and mysterious topic of suicide.

In 1935, I was a 16-year-old enthusiast, enrolled at UCLA. My favorite teacher was an assistant professor of psychology named Joseph Gengerelli. His favorites were Rene Descartes and John Stuart Mill. When he passed me on campus he would come up to me and put his face an inch or so from mine and say, "Shneidman, have you had any clear and distinct ideas?" Everybody knows Descartes' *Cogito ergo sum*, and I would say to him, "No sir, but if I do I'll come directly to you." He gave introspection a fulcrum place in any epistemology.

Gengerelli was also a keen believer in the importance of Mill's method of inductive science, how one gets from a number of particular observations—in nature, in the laboratory, in the clinic, even in the coroner's vault—to a reasonable inductive generalization. He taught me, and I learned it as only an eager adolescent can learn, Mill's canons, especially the method of difference, so that 15 years later—after a world war, marriage and fatherhood, a doctoral degree, and employment at a mental hospital—when I had occasion to go to the Los Angeles coroner's office for some information about two patients who had recently committed suicide, I was the beneficiary of Pasteur's dictum of chance and the prepared mind.

That fateful morning I descended into the coroner's vaults and found the folders for the two men. In the first folder, there was the expected grisly materials—a death certificate, an autopsy report, a police report, and photographs. But there was something I had never seen before—a suicide note. The second folder did not have a suicide note, but I stayed and looked at scores of folders that successive coroners had been keeping since early in the century.

When I saw that first suicide note there was a buzz in my ear and a voice that said, "Don't read it. Be able to state that you have not read this note. It is a genuine suicide note." And Mill's voice seemed to say to me, "The contrast with *genuine* notes is *simulated* suicide notes. You must somehow elicit suicide notes from nonsuicidal people." (And, over the following several months, with the help of Norman Farberow, that was done.) In the coroner's office where I was by chance that day, Mill (and my mind's previous preparation at the university) came to my side, figuratively speaking, reminded me of the practicability of the method of difference, and handed me a career. A scientific suicidology was born. I have stayed with the topic for over half a century. My writing this book—my latest and, realistically, perhaps my last—is an effort to share my enthusiasms and my insights, partly through the voices of others, with a new generation of would-be and working suicidologists.

I am now an octogenarian and feel an urgency to pass along my puzzlements and insights to everyone younger than I am—scientists, clinicians, students, former patients, survivors—who can profit from this intellectual and emotional journey, as I myself have profited from assembling this unusual travel brochure. My personal motivation in writing this book is, to my mind, quite simple: It is the wish to share. No writer or teacher —for that is how I see myself—thinks on paper without a potential readership in mind. I project the reader as someone like myself: Yearning to know more. Not surprisingly, I am personally acquainted with dozens of the hundred books on suicide currently listed in the computer printouts, but I hungered for a relatively simple, intellectually appealing volume that, in itself, would stimulate me to deeper and more practical understandings of suicidal phenomena. It did not exist; at least I could not find it. So I created it. I intend this book for people doing research on suicide, those helping to prevent suicide either through community intervention or engaged in clinical practice with suicidal persons, and other people who have touched suicide or who have been touched by it. In effect, a lot of people.

I need to say something about a section at the end of this book, "This I Believe." I had a serious debate with myself as to whether or not to include it. Part of me said that I should retain the omniscient objective voice and treat all 13 substantive chapters with equal weight (in my own somewhat wry and florid style) and not tip my hand as to what, after 80 years, I really believe. The other side of the argument said that if I took sides I ran the risk of disappointing (even alienating) some readers. But the winning inner hemisphere of my mind said that I owed it to my readers, who will have shared an intellectual journey with me, to tell them exactly where I stand. And that is what I have chosen to do. In any event, it is a lively debate that will keep the youngest of the readers cogitating until the middle of the 21st century, at least. And there is the additional bonus that it is a lien on my own post-self life.

ACKNOWLEDGMENTS

Grateful acknowledgments for permissions to reprint are made to the following individuals and publishers:

Chapter 1. From *History of Suicide: Voluntary Death in Western Culture* (pp. 94–97), by Georges Minois (Lydia G. Cochrane, Trans.), 1999, Baltimore: Johns Hopkins University Press. Copyright 1999. Reprinted with permission. (Originally published as *Histoire du Suicide*, Fayard, Libraire Artheme. Paris: 1996.)

Chapter 2. From *The Savage God: A Study of Suicide* (pp. 267–289), by A. Alvarez, 1971, New York: Random House. Copyright 1971—by A. Alvarez. Reprinted with permission of Gillon Aitken Associates Ltd.

Chapter 3. From *Suicide: A Study in Sociology*, pp. 259–276, by E. Durkheim (John A. Spaulding & George Simpson, Trans.), 1951, Glencoe, IL: Free Press. (Originally published as *Le Suicide: Etude de Sociologie*, 1897. Paris: Alcan.) © 1951, 1979. Reprinted with permission of The Free Press, a division of Simon & Schuster.

Chapter 4. From *Suicide: A Sociological and Statistical Study* (pp. 68–73), by L. I. Dublin, 1986, New York: Ronald Press Company. Reprinted with permission of the author's estate.

Chapter 5. From *The Thorn in the Chrysanthemum: Suicide and Economic Success in Modern Japan* (pp. 114–138), by M. Iga, 1986, Berkeley: University of California Press. Copyright 1986 The Regents of the University of California. Reprinted with permission.

Chapter 6. From "The Neurobiology of Suicide: From the Bench to the Clinic," by D. M. Stoff & J. J. Mann, 1997, New York: *Annals of the New York Academy of Sciences*, 836, pp. 1, 5–11. Copyright 1997 by the New York Academy of Sciences. Reprinted with permission.

Chapter 7. From *Man Against Himself* (pp. 318–336), by K. A. Menninger, 1938, New York: Harcourt, Brace. © 1938. Reprinted with permission of Harcourt, Inc.

Chapter 8. From *Suicides* (pp. 66–75), by J. Baechler (B. Cooper, Trans.), 1979. New York: Basic Books. Copyright 1979. Reprinted with permission of Persius Books. (Originally published as *Les Suicides*, 1975. Paris: Calman-Levy.)

Chapter 9. From *The Inman Diary*, by D. Aaron (Ed.), 1985, Cambridge, MA: Harvard University Press, two volumes, pages as noted in selection. Copyright 1985 by the President and Fellows of Harvard College. Reprinted with permission.

Chapter 10. From *Essential Papers on Suicide* (pp. 1–8), by J. T. Maltsberger & M. J. Goldblatt (Eds.), 1996, New York: New York University Press. Copyright 1996 by New York University Press. Reprinted with permission.

Chapter 11. From *Survivors of Suicide* (pp. 93–100), by A. C. Cain (Ed.), 1972, Springfield, IL: Charles C Thomas. (Albert C. Cain & Irene Fast, authors.) Copyright 1972 by Charles C Thomas. Reprinted with permission.

Chapter 12. From *The Samaritans: Befriending the Suicidal* (pp. 17–27, inclusive), by Chad Varah (Ed.), 1985, London: Constable & Robinson. Copyright 1985. Reprinted with permission.

Chapter 13. From *The Engima of Suicide* (pp. 329–331), by G. Howe Colt, 1991, New York: Summit Books. Copyright 1991 by George Howe Colt. Reprinted with permission of The Free Press, a division of Simon & Schuster, Inc.

COMPREHENDING
SUICIDE

INTRODUCTION

PLAN OF THE BOOK

From 1966 to 1969, when I was chief of the Center for the Study of Suicide Prevention at the National Institute of Mental Health in Bethesda, Maryland, a national center that supported research on suicide throughout the country, I made it a special point to see that all major legitimate points of view about suicide were represented in the government's largess. In my mind, the key word was "catholicity," that we would evenhandedly see that proponents of various theoretical points of view— sociological, psychological, epidemiological, historical, and biological—all found some place in the coveted list of awarded and funded grants. This same representativeness is the goal of this current volume. The 13 review chapters, each representing a previously published book, are subsumed under five overarching headings that, in their conglomerate, provide us with a comprehensive view of our topic. These five headings are Historical and Literary, Sociological, Biological, Psychiatric and Psychological, and Survivors and Volunteers.

There is an obvious multidimensionality to life. Whatever the mind is, it functions within a living brain. No brain, no mind. And that brain functions within a body that supports and feeds it, and that body, with its own history, operates within a culture. Think of walking through a large central square in some culturally rich old European city, and in the square there is the cathedral with its mores, the university with its library and its ties to the heritage of the past, the courts with their laws, the palace of justice, statues of the national heroes, the state opera, the national theater, the newspaper building, and the hall of records with family genealogies—all of the institutions that color and shape who a local citizen is and all of the beliefs, values, sentiments, and prejudices—including those about suicide—that person embodies. That is what these five categories are meant to reflect.

Each of the 13 chapters is divided into three parts: The first part of each chapter is an essay in which I have reviewed that book, put it in a larger context and, where possible, given some fresh (21st-century) slant to an old puzzle. The books range from almost brand new to over 100 years old. I do not see how any alert reader can peruse these books without a sharp and productive increase in comprehension of this mesmerizing topic. The second part is a reproduction of the title page and the table of contents of that book, so that the reader can see precisely what was in that book to get a feel for the book. And the third part of each chapter consists of a half dozen or so pages from the original text, reproduced verbatim.[1] These extended quotations are intended to give the reader authentic samples of the original author's own voice and glimpses into his style of writing and his methods of reasoning—*his* special way of comprehending suicide.

A few words about the selection of books might be in order. Why these? Of course, I gave much thought to "the list." I began with over two dozen possible selections. Immediately, I was constrained by the necessity to keep the printed volume to a manageable size. It was like fleeing a burning house. What to take? Once I had decided on the five main categories, the task became more focused. In general, I can say—without writing an apologia for the selection of each book—that I was guided by my desire to lead the reader (constantly in my mind) to certain books because they reflected my lifetime of study. If I may say so, I have the intuitive feel to know how to choose what to read and study in order to gain an in-depth and comprehensive understanding of suicide. I say to the reader, Trust me! If, in my convalescent home roomette—God save me from that fate—I am permitted to have only a dozen books on suicide on a small shelf for final contemplation, these dozen would be my choices, and, counting on the superintendent's benignity, there would be 13 for good measure, in addition, of course, to the books that I have myself written.

The not-so-hidden purpose of this book is to inflame the imagination and interest of each reader; to move the reader to seek out the original sources, to find—what? To find nuggets, solace, understanding, even tran-

---

[1] Throughout the 13 original texts, ellipses are used to indicate the omission of phrases, sentences, or paragraphs from the original text. Cross-references and some citations to other works, either in text or as a footnote, have been omitted without ellipses; where footnotes have been reproduced, I have kept the original numbering.

quility; to know that there is no simple answer to the enigma of suicide; to know that the end of each individual's universe is, like the universe itself, a gigantic jigsaw puzzle of a seemingly infinite number of pieces, many of which have dropped to the floor and have been swept under the cosmic rug.

A BRIEF HISTORY OF SUICIDE

Over the past two-plus millennia, one of the most persistent questions about suicide has not been when or how or even why but *where*? This is not a trivial question about the location of the death, but rather it concerns the *locus of blame*, the area of *conceptualization*. Our current popular discussions use words like *moralistic, sociological, medicalistic, existential*. There are dozens of books that address "the history of suicide," and I have selected one of the best of them by Georges Minois, a contemporary French scholar, to be included in this volume.

To my current way of thinking, the locus of conceptualization—the way in which the topic of suicide is "officially" seen by the state (the courts, the church, the press, the mores, society, the leading-edge intellectuals)—can be represented by a set of words ranging from *sin* to *selfhood*. Each of these views has had its brief decades or even centuries in the sun.

The historical story of the locus of suicide (in the Western world) can be told rather briefly. During classical Greek times, suicide was viewed in more than one way. It was tolerated and even lauded when done by patricians—generals and philosophers—but condemned if committed by plebians or slaves, whose labors were necessary for the smooth functioning of a patrician–slave society. In classical Rome, in the centuries just before the Christian era, life was held rather cheaply, and suicide was viewed rather neutrally or even positively. The Stoic philosopher Seneca (4 B.C.–69 A.D.) said,

> Living is not good, but living well. The wise man, therefore, lives as well as he should, not as long as he can. . . . He will always think of life in terms of quality not quantity. . . . Dying early or late is of no relevance, dying well or ill is . . . life is not to be bought at any cost.

In the early Christian era the excessive martyrdom and penchant toward suicide of early believers frightened church elders sufficiently for them to introduce a serious deterrent. That constraint was to relate suicide to crime and to the sin associated with that crime. A major change occurred in the 4th century with a categorical rejection of suicide by St. Augustine (354–430). Suicide was considered a crime because it precluded the possibility of repentance and because it violated the biblical Sixth Commandment relating to killing. Suicide was a greater sin than any sin one might wish to avoid. This view was elaborated by St. Thomas Aquinas (1225–1274), who emphasized that suicide was a mortal sin in that it usurped God's power over man's life and death. Neither the Old nor the New Testament directly forbids suicide, but by the year 700 the Catholic Church proclaimed that a person who attempted suicide was to be excommunicated. The notion of suicide as sin took firm hold and for hundreds of years thereafter played an important part in the Western view of self-destruction.

There is much to learn about the long stretch of several hundred years from 1000 A.D. to the 18th century, and much of it is explicated in the French historian and scholar Georges Minois's scholarly book entitled *History of Suicide* (1996). That book provides us with a segue to the French philosopher Jean Jacques Rousseau (1712–1778) who, by emphasizing the natural state of man, transferred sin from man to society, making people generally good and asserting that society makes them bad. The disputation as to the locus of blame—whether in people or in society—is a major tension that resonates throughout the history of suicidal thought. David Hume (1711–1776) was one of the first major Western philosophers to discuss suicide in the absence of the concept of sin. His famous essay "On Suicide," published in 1777, the year after his death, was promptly suppressed. That well-reasoned essay is a statement of the Enlightenment's position on suicide. The burden of the essay is to refute the view that suicide is a crime; it does so by arguing that suicide is not a transgression of our duties to God or to our fellow citizens or to ourselves. Hume states that

> prudence and courage should engage us to rid ourselves at once of existence when it becomes a burden. . . . If it be no crime in me to divert the Nile or Danube from its course, were I able to effect such purposes, where then is the crime in turning a few ounces of blood from their natural channel?

Whereas Hume tried to decriminalize suicide, Rousseau turned the blame from man to society.

In the 20th century, the two giants of suicidal theorizing—Emile Durkheim (1858–1917) in France and Sigmund Freud (1856–1939) in Austria—played rather different roles: Durkheim focused on society's inimical effects on the individual, while Freud, eschewing both the notions of sin and of crime, gave suicide back to man but put the locus of action in our unconscious mind.

Durkheim's best-known work *Le Suicide* in 1897 (although unavailable in English until 1951) established a model for sociological investigation of suicide. There have been many subsequent studies of this genre. The monographs and books on suicide by Ruth Cavan (Chicago, 1926), Calvin Schmidt (Seattle, 1928), Peter Sainsbury (London, 1955), and Henry and

Short (business cycles, 1954) all fall within the tradition of taking a plot of ground—a city or a country—and figuratively or literally reproducing its map several times to show its socially shady (and topographically shaded) areas, and their differential relationships to suicide rates. According to Durkheim, suicide is the result of society's strength or weakness of control over the individual. He posited three basic types of suicide, each a result of our relationship to society. In one instance, the "altruistic" suicide is literally required by that individual's society. Here, the customs or rules of the group demand suicide under certain circumstances. Hara-kiri and suttee are examples of altruistic suicide. In such instances, the person acted as though he had little choice. Self-inflicted death was honorable; continuing to live was ignominious. Society dictated a person's actions, and as individuals we are not strong enough to defy custom.

Most suicides in the United States are "egoistic"—Durkheim's second category. Contrary to the circumstances of an altruistic suicide, egoistic suicide occurs when the individual has too few ties with his or her community. Demands—in this case, to live—do not reach him or her. Proportionately, more unconnected individuals, especially men who are on their own—lonely old men—kill themselves than do people who are connected to church or family.

Finally, Durkheim called "anomic" those suicides that occurred when the accustomed relationship between an individual and society is suddenly shattered or disrupted. The shocking, immediate loss of a job or the death of a close friend or the loss of a fortune is thought sufficient to precipitate anomic suicide or, conversely, poor men surprised by sudden wealth have been shocked into anomic suicide. A situation of estrangement to one's usual ties to the habitual aspects of one's society is called *anomie*.

The students and followers of Durkheim include Maurice Halbwachs in France and Ronald Maris and Jack D. Douglas in the United States. Douglas, especially, argued that Durkheim's constructs came not so much from the facts of life and death as from official statistics that may have distorted those very facts that they are purported to report.

As Durkheim detailed the sociology of suicide, so Freud (although not writing directly on this topic) fathered psychological explanations. To him, suicide was essentially in the mind. Because individuals ambivalently identify with the objects of their own love, when they are frustrated the aggressive side of the ambivalence turns itself against the internalized person. The main psychoanalytical position on suicide was that it represented unconscious hostility directed toward the introjected ambivalently viewed love objects. For example, one killed oneself to murder the image of one's loved–hated father within one's breast. Psychodynamically, suicide was seen as murder in the 180th degree. Contemporary psychoanalysis has modified this view in a number of ways that extend the confines of this original prescription.

In an important exegesis of suicide, Robert E. Litman (1921–) traced the development of Freud's thoughts on this subject, taking into account Freud's clinical experiences and his changing theoretical positions from 1881 to 1939. It is evident from Litman's analysis that there are more factors to the psychodynamics of suicide than hostility. These factors include the general features of the human condition in Western civilization, specifically suicide-prone mechanisms involving rage, guilt, anxiety, dependency, and a great number of predisposing conditions. The feelings of helplessness, hopelessness, and abandonment are very important.

Psychodynamic explanations of suicide theory did not change too much from Freud to the American psychiatrist Karl Menninger (1893–1990). In his important 1938 book, *Man Against Himself*, Menninger, in captivating ordinary language, delineated the psychodynamics of hostility and asserted that the hostile drive in suicide is made up of three skeins: the wish to kill, the wish to be killed, and the wish to die. Gregory Zilboorg (1890–1959) refined this psychoanalytic hypothesis and stated that every suicidal case contained strong, unconscious hostility combined with an unusual lack of capacity to love others. He extended the locus of concern from solely intrapsychic dynamics to the external world and maintained that the role of a broken home in suicidal proneness demonstrated that both intrapsychic and external etiological elements were present.

In addition to the sociological and psychological approaches to the study of suicide, there is a contemporary thrust that might be called *philosophic* or *existential*. The French philosopher Albert Camus (1913–1960) begins his essay "The Myth of Sisyphus" (1942) by saying, "There is but one serious philosophic problem and that is suicide." The principal task of man is to respond to life's apparent meaninglessness; despair and its absurd quality. Ludwig Wittgenstein (1889–1951)—an Austrian born, English citizen—also stated that the main ethical issue for man is suicide. To Camus, Wittgenstein, and other philosophers, their ruminations were never meant as prescriptions for action.

There is yet another contemporary thread; it comes from the laboratory and has aspirations of being applicable in the clinic. It focuses both on the living and the dead brain and on such bodily fluids as blood and cerebrospinal fluid. It relates to the anatomy and physiology of suicide—the biological approach to the understanding of specific human behaviors.

The locus of conceptualization of suicide is set by the church, the government, books, mores, society, writers, and leading-edge intellectuals. It reflects the *zeitgeist*: the commonly held beliefs that are "in the air." Looking at this panorama of ideas and sentiments over the past millennium, it seems to me that a number of ideas have occupied intellectual space on the topic of suicide. Alliteratively, I call them sin, sacrilege, socius, soma, serum, psyche, and selfhood. Over the past 200 years, the main emphasis (and locus) for suicide has moved from accusations of sin toward efforts at compassion, understanding, and prevention. The *Encyclopedia Britannica* reflects these changes. My recent study[2] of the 14 separate articles on suicide in the various editions of the *Encyclopaedia* since 1777 (see the Epilogue) showed that society has moved light-years since the 18th-century excoriation of suicide as cowardly, sinful, and shameful to a contemporary emphasis on nurturance and support—like the Samaritans in Great Britain and the suicide prevention and hotline activities in the United States, whose interactions often begin with the question "How can we help you?"

This volume focuses on the 20th century and presents a panoply of important books representing various aspects of the current suicidological scene. In toto they reflect my own personal views, and I present them with pride and pleasure.

The list of 13 is meant—within the confines of this one slim volume—to be comprehensive and representative and to showcase some of the very best 20th-century books in the exciting field of suiciodology. I live with the hope that each person interested in suicide for whatever reason—scientist, clinician, health professional, volunteer, survivor, student, veteran or novice, concerned relative, or potential victim—will find stimulating entries in this volume, hints as to the mollification of suicide's dire consequences, and clues for its possible prevention.

---

[2] Shneidman, E. S. (1998). Suicide on my mind; *Britannica* on my table. *American Scholar, 67,* 93–104.

I

HISTORICAL AND LITERARY INSIGHTS

1

MINOIS
HISTORY OF SUICIDE: VOLUNTARY DEATH IN WESTERN CULTURE

Originally published in Paris, 1996

There is a special joy to the macrotemporal and macrospatial view, the sweep of history, the transcentury vista, time's Grand Canyon. This kind of interest accounts, in part, for the enthusiasm of history buffs.

In the 19th century especially, and particularly in France and England, the *scholarly* approach to suicide—to survey the past and report who had said what, and what thoughts had been put forward —pretty much constituted the study of suicide. The names of Donne, Burton, and Hume were well known. A typical 19th-century bibliography on suicide might include J. E. Esquirol, *Des Maladies Mentales Consideres Sous des Rapports Medieaux, Hygieniques et Medicologaux* (Paris, 1838); E. Morselli, *Il Suicidio* (Milano, 1879); A Legoyt, *Suicide Ancien et Modene* (Paris, 1881); W. W. Westcott, *Suicide, Its History, Literature, Jurisprudence, Causation and Prevention* (London, 1885); and S. A. K. Strahan, *Suicide and Insanity* (London, 1894). Nowadays, they all have a quaint, prescientific sound to them.

In our own time—1996 to be exact—Georges Minois, a French scholar and historian, has written a masterpiece in this genre. Minois's *Histoire du Suicide* is an encyclopedic tome in the tradition of the erudite French scholarship of Philipe Aries's *The Hour of Our Death*. Aries takes the topic of death from roughly the beginning of the Christian era to the year 1,000 A.D.; Minois considers the topic of suicide from around year 1,000 to the present. Both books are formidable exercises of the art of history.

The central words of Minois's book—he uses them several times —are Hamlet's "to be or not to be"; yes or no; light or total darkness; a dichotomous decision made "in the *mind*" (italics added). "The rest,"—the explication of suicide as a topic—is history. Minois's almost 400 wonderfully written pages are a telling of this history of suicide in the past millennium. The result is entertaining, engrossing, informative, enlightening, a first-rate scholarly "read."

As we see from the table of contents, the book is divided into the Middle Ages, the Renaissance, and the Enlightenment. Over these epochs, man—Western European man—changed. The mores changed, the technology—simple things like the saddle, stirrups, the eccentric, the crank—changed; the social order changed. Suicide changed. A 20th-century scientist once said that the plural of "anecdote" was "data;" surely, before that, the plural of anecdote was history, and that is what Minois provides us, hundreds and hundreds of anecdotes, places, names, church records, vignettes, bills of morality —all sorts of arcane and ordinary, recondite and recorded snippets of history, organized and arranged for our pleasure.

The study of history gives us a special sense of control. It organizes and puts a template on the past. This enables us to enjoy the paradox of understanding something better while at the same time not being able to do anything about it. (It is like pathology: A pathologist is a doctor who knows everything—but it's too late.) Yet, in our universal yearnings for understanding and control we gain some solace in being able to say "So that's the way it was?" Even more important is our capacity to say "So that is the route by which we arrived at our present state?" The real challenge—the *use* of history—is then to try to extrapolate forward and to venture how things might be in the future, specifically, in this case, how *suicide* might be conceptualized and responded to over the next few hundred years. What will the new vocabulary of suicide be? In terms of what concepts—not even thought of today—will "suicide"—if that's the term that will be used —be discussed? In this important enterprise, neologisms (and changing definitions) play an indispensable role; successive dictionaries, encyclopaedias, and cutting-edge textbooks provide the historical record.

If the full texts of all 13 books represented in this volume were ever put into one mammoth text, Minois's *History of Suicide* could nicely serve as the perfect prologue. In this same genre, I recently wrote an article[1] in which I traced the entries for "suicide" in the *Encyclopaedia Britannica* from 1777 to the present. Clearly, even in only the past 220 years, there have been radical changes in the connotative meanings of the suicidal act. Think, then, of the excitement of viewing the sweep of changes relating to suicide in the past 1,000 years, written in French ink, as though by a devoted monk, scribing with a condor's quill in a monastery on the highest hill in the country.

---

[1] Shneidman, E. S. (1998). Suicide on my mind; *Britannica* on my table, *American Scholar, 67,* 93–104.

HISTORY OF SUICIDE

Voluntary Death in Western Culture

GEORGES MINOIS

TRANSLATED BY
Lydia G. Cochrane

The Johns Hopkins University Press
BALTIMORE AND LONDON
[1996/1999]

CONTENTS

HISTORY OF SUICIDE

JOHN DONNE'S 'BIATHANATOS'

The point of arrival in this series of works on suicide, John Donne's *Biathanatos*, is an extraordinary book, especially when we consider that it was written around 1610 by an Anglican, chaplain to the king, who held a doctorate in divinity from Cambridge University and was a reader in divinity at Lincoln's Inn at the Inns of Court, London's great school of law. Donne was a humanist, a preacher, a theologian, a poet, and a man receptive to all the currents of thought of his age. Neither a marginal figure nor an eccentric, he was a responsible clergyman. That fact lends his treatise undeniable gravity.

Donne's somewhat embarrassed subtitle outlines his subject with a double negative: *A Declaration of that Paradoxe, or Thesis, that Selfe-homicide is not so naturally Sinne, that it may never be Otherwise.* In plain terms, in some cases suicide is justified. Donne's treatise was the first work wholly

---

From *History of Suicide: Voluntary Death in Western Culture* (pp. 94–97), by Georges Minois (Lydia G. Cochrane, Trans.), 1999, Baltimore: Johns Hopkins University Press. Copyright 1999. Reprinted with permission. (Originally published as *Histoire du Suicide*, Fayard, Libraire Artheme. Paris: 1996.)

I picked this particular selection from Minois's book largely because it refers to one of the most important early—17th-century—"philosophers of suicide," namely John Donne. In his 1644 *Biothanatos*, Donne "attempted to show that the condemnation of suicide derives from principles falsely considered to be self-evident and that 'self-homicide' is far from being the absolute sin that . . . theology made of it." Heretical stuff!

devoted to a rehabilitation of suicide. Donne was aware of his audacity and of his responsibility, and he came close to imitating Justus Lipsius and destroying his manuscript: "I have always gone so near suppressing it as that it is only not burnt," he wrote to Sir Robert Ker in 1619. He absolutely refused to have the work published, limiting himself to circulating copies among friends whom he could trust, and on the copy he left to his son he wrote, "Publish it not, do not print this, but yet burn it not." To Ker he wrote, "It is a book written by Jack Donne and not by Dr. Donne." The book had to wait until 1647, sixteen years after Donne's death, to be published. David Hume showed a like prudence in the eighteenth century when it came to his own treatise on suicide.

Prudence is not quite the right word. Donne was well aware that he was infringing a taboo, and he was afraid of having to take responsibility for suicides that might result from reading his book. It was one thing to profess admiration for Brutus and Cato, figures from so remote a past as to be nearly mythic; it was quite another thing to demonstrate that suicide is an act that does not violate natural or divine law, and thus one that should not be penalized. Donne takes his precautions: He insists that he is not writing a defense of suicide and refuses to specify the precise conditions under which suicide might be condoned. "I abstained purposely from extending this discourse to particular rules or instances, both because I dare not profess myself a master in so curious a science, and because the limits are obscure and steepy and slippery and narrow, and every error deadly, except where, a competent diligence being foreused, a mistaking in our conscious may prove an excuse." Donne complains earlier in the same work, however, that no one "brings the metal now to the touch," and he states that we must deliver "ourselves from the tyranny of this prejudice."

One of the cultural preoccupations of the times and a difficult personal situation converge in his thought. Donne felt himself a failure in his life, his marriage, and his career. He became melancholic and contemplated death, a theme that permeates his entire work. Despite the scholastic form Donne gave it, *Biathanatos* is not a stylistic exercise. Would he have taken so much trouble to write this treatise, then hide it, if it had been only an intellectual game? His book was rooted in both his life and his epoch: In the same years a young Catholic priest, Duvergier de Hauranne (later better known as Abbé de Saint-Cyran) also considered cases in which suicide might be an acceptable course, though with considerable less audacity than Donne.

One of Donne's most daring moves, and a point on which he broke with all previous interpretations of the question, was to treat suicide within the framework of Christian thought. Rather than choosing an indirect approach and reasoning from the examples of Cato, Lucretius, or Seneca, he places himself, from the outset, within Christian theology and uses only rational and religious arguments. His attack is frontal: We think it obvious that suicide is the worst of sins, but if we examine the arguments backing up that seemingly obvious tenet, we find that suicide might possibly not be a grave sin and perhaps not be a sin at all. In any event, we have no right to judge whether or not an individual is damned because he has killed himself, and many actions that we condemn today were authorized in the Bible.

In the three parts of *Biathanatos* Donne discusses whether suicide is contrary to the law of nature, to the law of reason, and to the law of God. If it is contrary to nature's law, we would have to condemn all mortification, all practices that aim at "taming" our nature. The nature that is unique to humankind is reason, which distinguishes us from the animals. Therefore reason should enlighten us about what is good or bad for us. It might at times be more reasonable to kill oneself. Moreover, people have killed themselves in all places and in all ages, which indicates that such an act is not so contrary to natural inclination as has been said.

The law of reason is what guides human laws. Certain laws, those of Rome in particular, do not condemn suicide, and canon law itself has not always condemned it. Certain theologians (St. Thomas Aquinas, for one) declare that suicide harms the state and society because it removes a useful member, but could not the same be said of a general who becomes a monk or of an émigré? Excessive mortification can be a kind of suicide in disguise, and no law condemns it. Thus we can renounce life for a higher good.

When he comes to God's law, Donne has no difficulty showing that no passage in the Bible condemns suicide. There is, of course, the Mosaic commandment against killing, but if exceptions are made for capital punishment and for the millions of homicides committed in times of war, why not make an exception for suicides, which are fewer in number? Is not voluntary martyrdom suicide? Was not the death of Christ, on the model of the Good Shepherd, suicide par excellence? St. Augustine's argument that Samson must have received a special command from God is pure supposition.

Donne's reasoning has its weak points; his style is heavy and tiresome; and he overuses syllogism and analogy. Still, his arguments are undeniably forceful.

JOHN DONNE, GALILEO'S CONTEMPORARY

In his *Biathanatos* Donne attempted to show that the condemnation of suicide derives from principles falsely considered to be self-evident, and that "self-homicide" is far from being the absolute sin that medieval and early modern theology made of it. Like hellebore, it was medicine "wholesome in desperate diseases, but otherwise poison." Once it was published long after Donne's death, *Biathanatos* met with little success, in part perhaps because its form put off readers, but even more because of its content. Few people were inclined to examine a book with such a sinister reputation: It scorched the hands even of those who shared its ideas but did not want to compromise themselves by citing it. A troublesome ally, *Biathanatos* was used only by a few libertines.

"To be or not to be?" was still the question, however. Any attempt to give too precise a response to it tended to break its spell, which resided in the melancholy and romantic vagueness that spun a mysterious fog over dizzying chasms that the mind sensed but could not clearly imagine. Donne took a step too far, daringly placing himself beyond what his times wanted to hear. His book nonetheless stands as striking testimony to an age that challenged traditional values and sought new guidelines. Like his exact contemporary, Pierre de Bérulle, Donne referred to the new astronomy of Copernicus, Giordano Bruno, and Galileo. The astronomical revolution left its mark on spirituality in the early seventeenth century; it helped to weaken traditional systems and to hasten the emergence of new certitudes in much the way that Einstein's theory of relativity turned culture and morality upside-down in the early twentieth century. During the same decade, from 1610 to 1620, Galileo (b. 1564) gave heliocentrism a scientific foundation; Pierre de Bérulle (b. 1575) elaborated a Christocentric spirituality founded in man's nothingness; Jakob Böhme (b. 1575) perfected a mysticism based on the "abyss" and on an opposition between being and nothingness—and Donne (b. 1572) asserted that human autonomy is sufficiently great to allow free choice between life and death. These events are more than pure coincidence; they indicate a cultural crisis that was to be resolved, temporarily at least, by the generation of Descartes, Pascal, and Hobbes.

2

ALVAREZ
THE SAVAGE GOD
A STUDY OF SUICIDE

Originally published in London, 1972

Alvarez's stimulating and informative book, *The Savage God*, is —as an extension of the author himself—an idiosyncratic book. A. Alvarez, an Englishman of Sephardic descent, is a poet, a poetry critic, an essayist, journalist and, in his own published words, "a failed suicide." On several grounds, he writes with unimpeachable authority.

Despite its virile title, *The Savage God* is a lyrical book. It presents us with a view of suicide "from a personal, literary and existential point of view." Among other things, it discusses self-destruction among artists, and it does this with beautifully drawn portraits of Dante, Cowper, Donne, Chatterton.

With high scholarship and palpable compassion, Alvarez makes the book like a seemless journey on which one sees the act of suicide as the end of a long experience relating to isolation and pain. Alvarez cannot help but speak as a poet and a sufferer of "the closed world of suicide with its own irresistible and fatal logic." His theme is that only from detailed case histories can "whatever theories and abstractions follow ... somehow be rooted in the human particular." The book radiates backward in history from his near death to his obsessions with the life and suicidal death of Sylvia Plath, the self-confessing American literary rocket, whom he knew personally, and Cesare Pavese, the Italian prize-winning writer, whose detailed lifelong diary he read carefully.

There is a section in the book about suicide *and* literature, which Alvarez carefully distinguishes from suicide *in* literature. He is interested in "the power that the act of suicide has exerted over the creative imagination." Under this heading, there is a focus on Dada and the self-destructive lives of the followers in literature, art, and drama of the European Dadaists, the near-nihilists, after World War I.

In his section on "Feelings," Alvarez describes

> a whole class of suicides . . . who take their own lives not in order to die, but to escape confusion, to clear their heads. They deliberately use suicide to create an unencumbered reality for themselves or to break through the patterns of obsession and necessity which they have unwittingly imposed on their lives.

For me, the key word in that chunk of wisdom is the verb *escape*. We shall see more of this concept in Baechler's book.

Alvarez concludes this beautiful book with an autobiographical Epilogue. Toward the very end of it he says,

> As for suicide: the sociologists and psychologists who talk of it as a disease puzzle me now as much as the Catholics and Muslims who call it the most deadly or mortal sins. It seems to me to be . . . a terrible but utterly natural reaction to the strained, narrow, unnatural necessities we sometimes create for outselves.

In sum, this book is a brilliant piece of 20th-century intellectual history seen from the point of view of a historian and a poet who has had a dear and talented friend commit suicide and has himself survived his own serious suicide attempt. There is no other book that combines breath-taking personal experience and scholarship in this way. *The Savage God* is an indispensable report by a uniquely prepared person, by fortune and misfortune, and is, in its entirety, a special gift to suicidology.

The Savage God

A Study of Suicide

by A. Alvarez

Random House 🏠 *New York*

[1971]

25

CONTENTS

THE SAVAGE GOD
EPILOGUE: LETTING GO

After all this, I have to admit that I am a failed suicide. It is a dismal confession to make, since nothing, really, would seem to be easier than to take your own life. Seneca, the final authority on the subject, pointed out disdainfully that the exits are everywhere: each precipice and river, each branch of each tree, every vein in your body will set you free. But in the event, this isn't so. No one is promiscuous in his way of dying. A man who has decided to hang himself will never jump in front of a train. And the more sophisticated and painless the method, the greater the chance of failure. I can vouch, at least, for that. I built up to the act carefully and for a long time, with a kind of blank pertinacity. It was the one constant focus of my life, making everything else irrelevant, a diversion. Each sporadic burst of work, each minor success and disappointment, each moment of calm and relaxation, seemed merely a temporary halt on my steady descent through layer after layer of depression, like an elevator stopping for a moment on the way down to the basement. At no point was there

From *The Savage God: A Study of Suicide* (pp. 267–289), by A. Alvarez, 1971, New York: Random House. Copyright 1971 by A. Alvarez. Reprinted with permission of Gillon Aitken Associates Ltd.

    I picked this particular selection from Alvarez's book because it is passionate, personal, illuminating, and wise—and it is my favorite section of that wise book.

any question of getting off or of changing the direction of the journey. Yet, despite all that, I never quite made it.

I see now that I had been incubating this death far longer than I recognized at the time. When I was a child, both my parents had half-heartedly put their heads in the gas oven. Or so they claimed. It seemed to me then a rather splendid gesture, though shrouded in mystery, a little area of veiled intensity, revealed only by hints and unexplained, swiftly suppressed outbursts. It was something hidden, attractive and not for the children, like sex. But it was also something that undoubtedly did happen to grownups. However hysterical or comic the behavior involved—and to a child it seemed more ludicrous than tragic to place your head in the greasy gas oven, like the Sunday roast joint—suicide was a fact, a subject that couldn't be denied; it was something, however awful, that people did. When my own time came, I did not have to discover it for myself.

. . .

. . . I went upstairs to the bathroom and swallowed forty-five sleeping pills. . . .

After that, I remember nothing at all until I woke up in the hospital and saw my wife's face swimming vaguely toward me through a yellowish fog. She was crying. But that was three days later, three days of oblivion, a hole in my head.

It happened ten years ago now, and only gradually have I been able to piece together the facts from hints and snippets, recalled reluctantly and with apologies. Nobody wants to remind an attempted suicide of his folly, or to be reminded of it. Tact and taste forbid. Or is it the failure itself which is embarrassing? Certainly, a successful suicide inspires no delicacy at all; everybody is in on the act at once with his own exclusive inside story. In my own case, my knowledge of what happened is partial and second-hand; the only accurate details are in the gloomy shorthand of the medical reports. Not that it matters, since none of it now means much to me personally. It is as though it had all happened to another person in another world.

. . .

The truth is, in some way I *had* died. The overintensity, the tiresome excess of sensitivity and self-consciousness, or arrogance and idealism, which came in adolescence and stayed on and on beyond their due time, like some visiting bore, had not survived the coma. It was as though I had finally, and sadly late in the day, lost my innocence. Like all young people, I had been high-minded and apologetic, full of enthusiasms I didn't quite mean and guilts I didn't understand. Because of them, I had forced my poor wife, who was far too young to know what was happening, into a spoiling, destructive role she had never sought. We had spent five years thrashing around in confusion, as drowning men pull each other under. Then I had lain for three days in abeyance, and awakened to feel nothing but a faint revulsion at everything and everyone. My weakened body, my thin breath, the slightest flicker of emotion filled me with distaste. I wanted only to be left to myself. Then, as the months passed, I began gradually to stir into another style of life, less theoretical, less optimistic, less vulnerable. I was ready for an insentient middle age.

Above all, I was disappointed. Somehow, I felt, death had let me down; I had expected more of it. I had looked for something overwhelming, an experience which would clarify all my confusions. But it turned out to be simply a denial of experience. All I knew of death were the terrifying dreams which came later. Blame it, perhaps, on my delayed adolescence: adolescents always expect too much; they want solutions to be immediate and neat, instead of gradual and incomplete. Or blame it on the cinema: secretly, I had thought death would be like the last reel of one of those old Hitchcock thrillers, when the hero relives as an adult that traumatic moment in childhood when the horror and splitting off took place; and thereby becomes free and at peace with himself. It is a well-established, much-imitated and persuasive formula. Hitchcock does it best, but he himself did not invent it; he was simply popularizing a new tradition of half-digested psychoanalytic talk about "abreaction," that crucial moment of cathartic truth when the complex is removed. Behind that is the old belief in last-moment revelations, deathbed conversions, and all those old wives' tales of the drowning man reliving his life as he goes down for the last time. Behind that again is an older tradition still: that of the Last Judgment and the afterlife. We all expect something of death, even if it's only damnation.

But all I had got was oblivion. . . .

I thought death would be like that: a synoptic vision of life, crisis by crisis, all suddenly explained, justified, redeemed, a Last Judgment in the coils and circuits of the brain. Instead, all I got was a hole in the head, a round zero, nothing. I'd been swindled.

Months later I began to understand that I had had my answer, after all. The despair that had led me to try to kill myself had been pure and unadulterated, like the final, unanswerable despair a child feels, with no before or after. And childishly, I had expected death not merely to end it but also to explain it. Then, when death let me down, I gradually saw that I had been using the wrong language; I had translated the thing into Americanese. Too many movies, too many novels, too many trips to the States had switched my understanding into a hopeful, alien tongue. I no longer thought of myself as unhappy; instead, I had "problems." Which is an optimistic way of putting it, since problems imply solutions, whereas unhappiness is merely a condition of life which you must live with, like the weather. Once I had accepted that there weren't ever going to be any answers, even in death, I found to my surprise that I didn't much care whether I was happy or unhappy; "problems" and "the problem of problems" no longer existed. And that in itself is already the beginning of happiness.

It seems ludicrous now to have learned something so obvious in such a hard way, to have had to go almost the whole way into death in order to grow up. Somewhere, I still feel cheated and aggrieved, and also ashamed of my stupidity. Yet, in the end, even oblivion was an experience of a kind. Certainly, nothing has been quite the same since I discovered for myself, in my own body and on my own nerves, that death is simply an end, a dead end, no more, no less. And I wonder if that piece of knowledge isn't in itself a form of death. After all, the youth who swallowed the sleeping pills and the man who survived are so utterly different that someone or something must have died. Before the pills was another life, another person altogether, whom I scarcely recognize and don't much like—although I suspect that he was, in his priggish way, far more likable than I could ever be. Meanwhile, his fury and despair seem improbable now, sad and oddly diminished.

. . .

As for suicide: the sociologists and psychologists who talk of it as a disease puzzle me now as much as the Catholics and Muslims who call it the most deadly of mortal sins. It seems to me to be somehow as much beyond social or psychic prophylaxis as it is beyond morality, a terrible but utterly natural reaction to the strained, narrow, unnatural necessities we sometimes create for ourselves. And it is not for me. Perhaps I am no longer optimistic enough. I assume now that death, when it finally comes, will probably be nastier than suicide, and certainly a great deal less convenient.

II

SOCIOLOGICAL INSIGHTS

3

DURKHEIM
SUICIDE: A STUDY IN SOCIOLOGY

Originally published in Paris, 1897

In the 18th and 19th centuries, the notions of political arithmetic, of statistics, of the symmetry and power of numbers were in the air. In 1741, the science of statistics as it is known today came into existence with the work of Sussmilch, a Prussian clergyman who made a systematic attempt to correlate "political arithmetic," or what we now call "vital statistics." ("Statistics" referred to the "istics" of the state.) From this study came what was subsequently called the "laws of large numbers," which permitted extended use of what earlier has simply been crude data (like John Graunt's London bills of mortality about deaths during the London plague). These numbers about deaths and births could supply important data for coffin makers, tax collectors, military recruiters, government planners—those throughout Europe as well as in the American colonies. James H. Cassedy, in 1969, in *Demography in Early America*, said that Sussmilch's analysis of vital data from church registers became the ultimate scientific demonstration of the regularity of God's demographic laws. And God's demographic laws were quickly secularized: In the eighth edition of the *Encyclopaedia Britannica* in 1852, Henry Thomas Buckle, the English chess prodigy and scientifically minded historian, wrote that "su-

icide is merely the product of the general condition of society . . .
[thus] we are able to predict within a small limit of error the number
of voluntary deaths for each ensuring period. . . ."

Demography was in the air.

Emile Durkheim (1858–1917) is the best-known name in all of
academic suicidology. Nowadays, his book *Le Suicide*, written in 1897
but amazingly not translated into English until 1951, is the best-known
text (by name if not by content) in the field. He is honored for having
explicated his sociological method and applied it to the topic of suicide. The method involves taking a large plot of land, a political entity,
usually a country although a large city will do, and literally shading it
in terms of its ordinary and shady demographic facts such as sex, age,
marital status, socioeconomic level, and so on, and relating those figures to some aberrant or problematic dependent variable. Many contemporary sociological scholars believe that Durkheim might have
written a sociological masterpiece on crime, or prostitution, or alcoholism (rather than suicide); that his book is more a demonstration
of the power of the *method* than essentially a treatise on that topic.
But suicide has the scientific advantage that, compared to other social
maladies, it, the *act*, is undeniably more clear cut and more subject
to interreporter agreement. The brilliant criticisms of Durkheim's
work by American sociologist Jack Douglas in the 1960s focused on
the questionable reliabilities of the official reporting—underreporting
—of suicidal deaths that Durkheim used, that is, the unscientific nature of Durkheim's raw data. But Durkheim's triumph remains: to
combine empirical research with sociological theory. It was what
Durkheim made of the different shadings in the data, the "social
facts," that excited the intellectual community.

Every social science undergraduate knows Durkheim's three
main types of suicide (there is a fourth): (a) *egoistic suicide*, which
may result when an individual shuts himself or herself off from other
human beings; (b) *altruistic suicide*, which may stem from great loy-
alty, fealty, or identification with the rules and mores of a society; and
(c) *anomic suicide*, which may come from the perception that one's
relationship to one's society—the social world—has radically
changed, like suddenly becoming very poor—or, conversely, suddenly
being elevated or successful or rich. *Anomie*, the feeling of estrangement from one's roots or one's fellows has, in the past hundred years,
been analyzed as a root cause of 20th-century bitterness and affect-
lessness, especially by the Ishmaels of the world. Parts of Durkheim
were absorbed by the Camus-minded thinkers, especially in Europe.
But the central glue of Durkheim's sociological theorizing lay in the
interstice between the individual and that individual's society. There
is a subtle but important difference between saying that an individual

is depressed and rejected and an individual feels estranged from his or her society. Durkheim did not just look at the data; he transmuted them into sociological magic by radically reclassifying their internal implications.

I had read and reread portions of Durkheim's book over the past half-century and, for me, there was always something puzzling about its aura. I had an inchoate feeling about the *style* of the whole book. Something troubled me because it had a whiff of familiarity that I could not identify. And then somewhere I read the openly known fact that Durkheim, although not himself religious as an adult, was the son of a rabbi and the grandson of rabbis. And then, the feeling of the book, its style of argument came to me. Durkheim explicates. He discusses and unfolds the meaning of his original ideas. And when you think he must be done, it turns out that that is just the 7th inning stretch; there are innings to go. He says it, he says it again, and then he turns it another way and says it. And then, after you think that you finally understand what he wants you to know, he says, *"But on the other hand. . . ."* Durkheim is a Yeshiva bucher! *Le Suicide* is a Talmudic document. That, in my opinion, accounts for some of its mysterious, murky, open-ended, profound, and endlessly fascinating quality. All the other dozen books in this volume are good books, landmark books; some perhaps are great books, but only *Le Suicide* is a Mishnah.

Suicide

A STUDY IN SOCIOLOGY

By Emile Durkheim

TRANSLATED BY JOHN A. SPAULDING AND GEORGE SIMPSON
EDITED WITH AN INTRODUCTION BY GEORGE SIMPSON
THE FREE PRESS OF GLENCOE

[1897/1951]

CONTENTS

SUICIDE: A STUDY IN SOCIOLOGY BOOK TWO, CHAPTER 5, SECTION IV, PAGE 403.

But economic anomy is not the only anomy which may give rise to suicide.

The suicides occurring at the crisis of widowhood, of which we have already spoken, are really due to domestic anomy resulting from the death of husband or wife. A family catastrophe occurs which affects the survivor. He is not adapted to the new situation in which he finds himself and accordingly offers less resistance to suicide.

But another variety of anomic suicide should draw greater attention,

From *Suicide: A Study in Sociology*, pp. 259–276, by E. Durkheim (John A. Spaulding and George Simpson, Trans.), 1951. Glencoe, IL: Free Press. (Originally published as *Le Suicide: Etude de Sociologie*, 1897. Paris: Alcan.) © 1951, 1979. Reprinted with permission of The Free Press, a division of Simon & Schuster.

I picked this particular selection from Durkheim's seminal book because it touches on "conjugal anomy" and thus is of special interest to all of us today who are concerned with marriage, divorce, single parenthood, women's liberation, and patterns of dyadic coupling.

This selection is an extended essay about marriage and suicide. In Durkheim's Detailed Table of Contents (at the end of his book), he writes the following about this section: "Suicide due to conjugal anomy. Widowhood. Divorce. Parallelism between divorces and suicides. . . . The weakening of matrimonial discipline implicit in divorce aggravates the tendency of men to suicide and diminishes that of women. . . . Conception of marriage emerging from this chapter."

TABLE XXV
Comparison of European States from the Point of View of Both Divorce and Suicide

	Annual Divorces per 1,000 Marriages	Suicides per Million Inhabitants
I. COUNTRIES WHERE DIVORCE AND SEPARATION ARE RARE		
Norway	0.54 (1875–80)	73
Russia	1.6 (1871–77)	30
England and Wales	1.3 (1871–79)	68
Scotland	2.1 (1871–81)	. . .
Italy	3.05 (1871–73)	31
Finland	3.9 (1875–79)	30.8
Averages	2.07	46.5
II. COUNTRIES WHERE DIVORCE AND SEPARATION ARE OF AVERAGE FREQUENCY		
Bavaria	5.0 (1881)	90.5
Belgium	5.1 (1871–80)	68.5
Holland	6.0 (1871–80)	35.5
Sweden	6.4 (1871–80)	81
Baden	6.5 (1874–79)	156.6
France	7.5 (1871–79)	150
Wurttemberg	8.4 (1876–78)	162.4
Prussia	. . .	133
Averages	6.4	109.6
III. COUNTRIES WHERE DIVORCE AND SEPARATION ARE FREQUENT		
Kingdom of Saxony	26.9 (1876–80)	299
Denmark	38 (1871–80)	258
Switzerland	47 (1876–80)	216
Averages	37.3	257

both because it is more chronic and because it will serve to illustrate the nature and functions of marriage.

In the *Annales de demographie internationale* (September 1882), Bertillon published a remarkable study of divorce, in which he proved the following proposition: throughout Europe the number of suicides varies with that of divorces and separations.

If the different countries are compared from this twofold point of view, this parallelism is apparent. Not only is the relation between the averages evident, but the single irregular detail of any importance is that of Holland, where suicides are not as frequent as divorces.

The law may be yet more vigorously verified if we compare not different countries but different provinces of a single country. Notably, in

TABLE XXVI
Comparison of Swiss Cantons from the Point of View of Divorce and Suicide

	Divorces and Separations per 1,000 Marriages	Suicides per Million		Divorces and Separations per 1,000 Marriages	Suicides per Million
I. CATHOLIC CANTONS					
French and Italian					
Tessino	7.6	57	Freiburg	15.9	119
Valais	4.0	47			
Averages	5.8	50	Averages	15.9	119
German					
Uri	. . .	60	Solothurn	37.7	205
Upper Unterwalden	4.9	20	Inner Appenzell	18.9	158
Lower Unterwalden	5.2	1	Zug	14.8	87
Schwyz	5.6	70	Luzern	13.0	100
Averages	3.9	37.7	Averages	21.1	137.5
II. PROTEST CANTONS					
French					
Neufchâtel	42.4	560	Vaud	43.5	352
German					
Bern	47.2	229	Schaffhausen	106.0	602
Basel (city)	34.5	323	Outer Appenzell	100.7	213
Basel (country)	33.0	288	Glaris	83.1	127
			Zurich	80.0	288
Averages	38.2	280	Averages	92.4	307
III. CANTONS MIXED AS TO RELIGION					
Argau	40.0	195	Geneva	70.5	360
Grisons	30.9	116	Saint Gall	57.6	179
Averages	36.9	155	Averages	64.0	269

Switzerland the agreement between the two series of phenomena is striking. The Protestant cantons have the most divorces and also the most suicides. The mixed cantons follow, from both points of view, and only then come the Catholic cantons. Within each group the same agreements appear. Among the Catholic cantons Solothurn and Inner Appenzell are marked by the high number of their divorces; they are likewise marked by the number of their suicides. Freiburg, although Catholic and French, has a considerable number of both divorces and suicides. Among the Protestant German cantons none has so many divorces as Schaffhausen; Schaffhausen also leads the list of suicides. Finally, the mixed cantons, with the one exception of Argau, are classed in exactly the same way in both respects.

The same comparison, if made between French departments, gives the same result. Having classified them in eight categories according to the importance of their suicidal mortality, we discovered that the groups thus formed were arranged in the same order as with reference to divorces and separations:

	Suicides per Million		Average of Divorces and Separations per 1,000 Marriages
1st group (5 departments)	Below	50	2.6
2nd group (18 departments)	From	51 to 75	2.9
3rd group (15 departments)		76 to 100	5.0
4th group (19 departments)		101 to 150	5.4
5th group (10 departments)		151 to 200	7.5
6th group (9 departments)		201 to 250	8.2
7th group (4 departments)		251 to 300	10.0
8th group (5 departments)	Above	300	12.4

Having shown this relation, let us try to explain it.

We shall mention only as a note the explanation Bertillon summarily suggested. According to that author, the number of suicides and that of divorces vary in parallel manner because both depend on the same factor: the greater or less frequency of people with unstable equilibrium. There are actually, he says, more divorces in a country the more incompatible married couples it contains. The latter are recruited especially from among people of irregular lives, persons of poor character and intelligence, whom this temperament predisposes to suicide. The parallelism would then be due, not to the influence of divorce itself upon suicide, but to the fact that these two phenomena derive from a similar cause which they express differently. But this association of divorce with certain psychopathic flaws is made arbitrarily and without proof. There is no reason to think that there are 15 times as many unbalanced people in Switzerland as in Italy and from 6 to 7 times as many in France, and yet in the first of these countries divorces are 15 times as frequent as in the second and about 7 times as frequent as in the third. Moreover, so far as suicide is concerned, we know how far purely individual conditions are from accounting for it. Furthermore, all that follows will show the inadequacy of this theory.

One must seek the cause of this remarkable relation, not in the organic predispositions of people but in the intrinsic nature of divorce. As our first proposition here we may assert: in all countries for which we have the necessary data, suicides of divorced people are immensely more numerous than those of other portions of the population.

	Suicides in a Million							
	Unmarried Above 15 Years		Married		Widowed		Divorced	
	Men	Women	Men	Women	Men	Women	Men	Women
Prussia (1887–1889)*	360	120	430	90	1,471	215	1,875	290
Prussia (1883–1890)*	388	129	498	100	1,552	194	1,952	328
Baden (1885–1893)	458	93	460	85	1,172	171	1,328	. . .
Saxony (1847–1858)	. . .	. . .	481	120	1,242	240	3,102	312
Saxony (1876)	555.18†		821	146	. . .	. . .	3,252	389
Wurttemberg (1846–1860)	. . .	. . .	226	52	530	97	1,298	281
Wurttemberg (1873–1892)	251	. . .	218†		405†		796†	

*There appears to be some error in the figures for Prussia here.—Ed
†Men and women combined.—Ed.

Thus, divorced persons of both sexes kill themselves between three and four times as often as married persons, although younger (40 years in France as against 46 years), and considerably more often than widowed persons in spite of the aggravation resulting for the latter from their advanced age. What is the explanation?

There is no doubt that the change of moral and material regimen which is a consequence of divorce is of some account in this result. But it does not sufficiently explain the matter. Widowhood is indeed as complete a disturbance of existence as divorce; it usually even has much more unhappy results, since it was not desired by husband and wife, while divorce is usually a deliverance for both. Yet divorced persons who, considering their age, should commit suicide only one half as often as widowed persons, do so more often everywhere, even twice as often in certain countries. This aggravation, to be represented by a coefficient between 2.5 and 4, does not depend on their changed condition in any way.

Let us refer to one of the propositions established above to discover the causes of this fact. In the third chapter of Book II, we saw that in a given society the tendency of widowed persons to suicide was a function of the corresponding tendency of married persons. While the latter are highly protected, the former enjoy an immunity less, to be sure, but still considerable, and the sex best protected by marriage is also that best protected in the state of widowhood. Briefly, when conjugal society is dissolved by the death of one of the couple, the effects which it has with reference to suicide continue to be felt in part by the survivor. Then, however, is it not to be supposed that the same thing takes place when the marriage is interrupted, not by death, but by a judicial act, and that the aggravation which afflicts divorced persons is a result not of the divorce but of the marriage ended by divorce? It must be connected with some quality of the matrimonial society, the influence of which the couple continue to experience even when separated. If they have so strong an inclination to suicide, it is because they were already strongly inclined to it while living together and by the very effect of their common life.

Admitting so much, the correspondence between divorces and suicides becomes explicable. Actually, among the people where divorce is common, this peculiar effect of marriage in which divorce shares must necessarily be very wide-spread; for it is not confined to households predestined to legal separation. If it reaches its maximum intensity among them, it must also be found among the others, or the majority of the others, though to a lesser degree. For just as where there are many suicides, there are many attempted suicides, and just as mortality cannot grow without morbidity increasing simultaneously, so wherever there are many actual divorces there must be many households more or less close to divorce. The number of actual divorces cannot rise, accordingly, without the family condition predisposing to suicide also developing and becoming general in the same degree, and thus the two phenomena naturally vary in the same general direction.

Not only does this hypothesis agree with everything demonstrated above but it is susceptible of direct proof. Indeed, if it is well-founded, married persons in countries where divorces are numerous must have less immunity against suicide than where marriage is indissoluble. This is the net result of the facts, at least *so far as husbands are concerned* as appears from Table XXVII on the following page. Italy, a Catholic country in which divorce is unknown, is also the country with the highest coefficient of preservation for husbands; it is less in France, where separations have always been more frequent, and can be seen to diminish as we pass to countries where divorce is more widely practiced.[13]

. . .

While this explanation accounts both for the observed parallelism between divorces and suicides[20] and the inverse variations shown by the immunity of husband and that of the wife, it is confirmed by several other facts:

1. Only where divorce applies, can there be real matrimonial instability; for it alone completely severs marriage, whereas separation merely

---

[13] If we compare only these few countries from this point of view, it is because statistics for the others combine the suicides of husbands with those of wives; and we shall see below how imperative it is to keep them separate.

But one should not conclude from this table that in Prussia, Baden and Saxony husbands really kill themselves more than unmarried men. We must not forget that these coefficients were compiled independently of age and of its influence on suicide. Now, as men of the average age of the unmarried, or from 25 to 30 years, commit suicide about half as often as men of 40 to 45 years, the average age for husbands, the latter enjoy some immunity even in countries with frequent divorce; but it is less than elsewhere. . . .

[20] Since the wife's immunity is greater where the husband's is less, it may seem strange that there is no compensation. But as the wife's share in the total number of suicides is very slight, the decrease in female suicides is imperceptible in the whole and does not balance the increase of male suicides. Thus divorce is ultimately associated with a rise in the total number of suicides.

44

TABLE XXVII
Influence of Divorce on the Immunity of Married Persons

Country	Suicides per Million Persons		Coefficient of Preservation of Married with Reference to Unmarried Men
	Unmarried Men Above 15 Years	Married Men	
Where divorce does not exist			
Italy (1884–88)	145	88	1.64
France (1863–68)*	273	245.7	1.11
Where divorce is common			
Baden (1885–93)	458	460	0.99
Prussia (1883–90)	388	498	0.77
Prussia (1887–89)	364	431	0.83

	Per one hundred suicides of every marital status.		
Where divorce is very frequent†	Unmarried men	Married men	
	27.5	52.5	0.63
Saxony (1879–80)	Per one Hundred male inhabitants of every marital status.		
	Unmarried men	Married men	
	42.10	52.47	

*We take this distant period because divorce did not exist at all at the time. The law of 1884 re-establishing it seems, however, up to the present, to have had no perceptible effects on the suicides of married men; their coefficient of preservation had not appreciably changed in 1888–92; an institution does not produce its effects in so short a time.

†For Saxony we have only the relative numbers given above and taken from Oettingen; they are enough for the purpose. In Legoyt (p. 171) other data will be found likewise proving that in Saxony married persons have a higher rate than unmarried. Legoyt himself notes this with surprise.

partially suspends certain of its effects without giving the couple their liberty. If, then, this special anomy really increases the suicidal tendency, divorced people should have a far higher aptitude than those merely separated. This is in fact the gist of the only document on this matter known to use. According to a calculation by Legoyt, in Saxony, during the period 1847–56, there were, as an annual average, 1,400 suicides for a million divorced persons and only 176 for a million separated persons. This latter rate is even below that of husbands (318).

2. If the strong suicidal tendency of the unmarried is partially connected with the sexual anomy in which they chronically exist, the aggravation they suffer must be most perceptible just when sexual feelings are most aroused. And in fact, the suicide rate of the unmarried grows between 20 and 45 years much more rapidly than after that; it quadruples during this period, while from 45 to the maximum age (after 80 years) it only

doubles. But no such acceleration appears among women; the rate of unmarried women does not even double from 20 to 45 years, but merely rises from 106 to 171. The sexual period therefore does not affect the increase of female suicides. This is just what we should expect if, as we have granted, woman is not very sensitive to this form of anomy.

3. Finally, several facts established in Chapter III of this very book are explained by the theory just set forth and consequently help to verify it.

We saw in that chapter that marriage in France, by itself and irrespective of family, gives man a coefficient of preservation of 1.5. We know now to what this coefficient corresponds. It represents the advantages obtained by a man from the regulative influence exerted upon him by marriage, from the moderation it imposes on his inclinations and from his consequent moral well-being. But at the same time we noted that in the same country the condition of a married woman was, on the contrary, made worse with respect to suicide unless the advent of children corrects the ill effects of marriage for her. We have just stated the reason. Not that man is naturally a wicked and egoistic being whose role in a household is to make his companion suffer. But in France where, until recently, marriage was not weakened by divorce, the inflexible rule it imposed on women was a very heavy, profitless yoke for them. Speaking generally, we now have the cause of that antagonism of the sexes which prevents marriage favoring them equally: their interests are contrary; one needs restraint and the other liberty.

Furthermore, it does seem that at a certain time of life man is affected by marriage in the same way as woman, though for different reasons. If, as we have shown, very young husbands kill themselves much more often than unmarried men of the same age, it is doubtless because their passions are too vehement at that period and too self-confident to be subjected to so severe a rule. Accordingly, this rule seems to them an unendurable obstacle against which their desire dashes and is broken. This is probably why marriage produces all its beneficent effects only when age, supervening, tempers man somewhat and makes him feel the need of discipline.[23]

Finally, in this same Chapter III we saw that where marriage favors the wife rather than the husband, the difference between the sexes is always

---

[23] It is even probable that marriage in itself produces a prophylactic effect only later, after the age of thirty. Actually, until that age, childless married men commit as many suicides in absolute numbers as married men with children, 6.6 from 20 to 25 years, for both, and from 25 to 30 years, 33 for the former and 34 for the latter. Of course, however, marriages with children are much more common than infertile marriages at this period. The tendency of the husbands of the latter marriages to suicide must therefore be several times as strong as that of husbands with children; or very close in intensity to that of unmarried men. Unfortunately we can only form hypotheses on the subject; for, as the census does not give the population of husbands without children for each age, as distinct from husbands with children, we cannot calculate separately the rate of each for each period of life. We can give only the absolute numbers. . . .

less than when the reverse is true. This proves that, even in those societies where the status of matrimony is wholly in the woman's favor, it does her less service than it does man where it is he that profits more by it. Woman can suffer more from marriage if it is unfavorable to her than she can benefit by it if it conforms to her interest. This is because she has less need of it. This is the assumption of the theory just set forth. The results obtained previously and those arising from the present chapter therefore combine and check each other mutually.

Thus we reach a conclusion quite different from the current idea of marriage and its role. It is supposed to have been originated for the wife, to protect her weakness against masculine caprice. Monogamy, especially, is often represented as a sacrifice made by man of his polygamous instincts, to raise and improve woman's condition in marriage. Actually, whatever historical causes may have made him accept this restriction, he benefits more by it. The liberty he thus renounces could only be a source of torment to him. Woman did not have the same reasons to abandon it and, in this sense, we may say that by submitting to the same rule, it was she who made a sacrifice.[25]

---

[25] The above considerations show that there is a type of suicide the opposite of anomic suicide, just as egoistic and altruistic suicides are opposites. It is the suicide deriving from excessive regulation, that of persons with futures pitilessly blocked and passions violently choked by oppressive discipline. It is the suicide of very young husbands, of the married woman who is childless. So, for completeness' sake, we should set up a fourth suicidal type. But it has so little contemporary importance and examples are so hard to find aside from the cases just mentioned that it seems useless to dwell upon it. However it might be said to have historical interest. Do not the suicides of slaves, said to be frequent under certain conditions, belong to this type, or all suicides attributable to excessive physical or moral despotism? To bring out the ineluctible and inflexible nature of a rule against which there is no appeal, and in contrast with the expression "anomy" which has just been used, we might call it *fatalistic suicide*.

4

DUBLIN
SUICIDE: A SOCIOLOGICAL AND STATISTICAL STUDY

Originally published in New York, 1968

Louis I. Dublin received his PhD from Columbia University in 1904. He soon joined the Metropolitan Life Insurance Company and, in 1909, established a statistical bureau. After a long and successful career he retired in 1952 as second vice president and statistician of that company. In addition to his books—*To Be or Not to Be, The Money Value of a Man*, and *Length of Life*—he has written over 600 articles and addresses in the fields of public health, vital statistics, and demography.

In the past half century, the two American classics on suicide have been Karl Menninger's *Man Against Himself* (1938) and Louis Dublin's *To Be or Not to Be* (1933), books widely apart in genre, each deserving its own wide reputation.

Menninger's book enunciates a theoretical position (largely relating to Eros and Thanatos), which is still in print today. More than that, it introduced psychodynamic theory, specifically as related to

This review adapted from a review, by E. S. Shneidman, 1964, *Contemporary Psychology*, 9, pp. 370–371. Copyright 1964 by the American Psychological Association. Reproduced with permission.

inimical and self-destructive behaviors, to every literate person in the land.

Dublin's *To Be or Not to Be*, published in 1933, was for many the equivalent of the *Encyclopaedia Britannica* of suicide, the one reliable source for background facts and figures. Logos, not Thanatos or Eros, was his totem. *Suicide: A Sociological and Statistical Study*, Dublin's updating of his earlier book, is as welcome as a new encyclopedic supplement to the proud owner of the 1933 edition. Dublin has done a marvelous temporal refurbishment, bringing his work up-to-date, retaining what was meaningful, and reflecting with solid scholarship what is useful in the then-current (1960s) suicidal scene.

In comparison with his earlier book (*To Be or Not to Be*), this new book—a rewriting too extensive to call it merely a revision—is shorter (and more pithy) and, at the same time, more wide ranged and filled with deeper distillations of thought.

The book contains 21 chapters divided among five parts: "People Who Commit Suicide," "The Setting of Suicide," "The History of Suicide"—a book in itself, "Psychological Aspects of Suicide" (including emotional factors in suicide and mental disease in suicide), and "Toward the Conquest of Suicide" (with a fine chapter describing current suicide prevention centers). There are many bonuses in this book, even beyond the sociological and statistical presentations and summaries. For my part, I like Dublin best when he rumbles in his wonderfully mature and moral way, commenting on trust and faith.

This book contains wonderful surprises, all the more delightful for their being unexpected. Here is a book supposedly devoted to precise statistics. (It is said that as the statistician of a huge life insurance company, Dublin was interested not only in pennies but also in mills; savings of millions of mills—based on precise actuarial tables—resulted in profits of thousands of dollars.) In *Suicide*, Dublin favors us with a concise four-page résumé of the best 19th-century references on suicide, followed immediately by a brief essay on America's foremost psychologist–philosopher William James:

> The positive message of religion to William James is the belief in the existence of an unseen order of some sort in which the riddles of the natural order may be explained. To paraphrase his thinking: The physical order of nature does not reveal any harmonious spiritual intent, and so we have a right to supplement what we see by an unseen spiritual order which we assume on trust. We cannot escape the conclusion that the science we know is but a drop, our ignorance is a sea; certainly the world of our present natural knowledge is enveloped in a larger world of some sort, of whose property we at present can frame no idea. It is a fact of human nature that man can live and die by the help of a sort of

faith that goes without a single dogma or definition. If you destroy the assurance that there is some law and order in the universe beyond our comprehension, all the light and radiance of existence are extinguished. Often the suicidal mood will then set in. Frequently faith is the only thing that makes life worth living; if you refuse to believe you may indeed be right, but at the same time you may perhaps irretrievably perish. If you surrender to the nightmare view of life and crown your unbelief by your own suicide you have indeed made a picture totally black. Your mistrust of life has removed whatever worth your own enduring experience might have given to it. Then his final challenge re: "Be not afraid of life! Believe that life is worth living and your belief will help create the fact." No message could be nobler than these words of a great thinker and scientist. (p. 135)

Dublin feels that we do not yet have enough facts—"we must wait further accumulation and analysis of data"—for major theorizing about the etiological formulae of suicidal phenomena. That's an opinion, and he is more entitled to his opinion in this field than almost anybody. (In the famous 1910 session on suicide in Vienna, Freud said, at the conclusion of that meeting; "Let us suspend our judgment until experience has solved this problem.") Even so, I would have been especially pleased to have had Dublin's thoughts about the definitions and meanings of "suicide" and by his discussion of the problems involved in the certification of death and the methodological issues imbedded in interpreting interclass, interstate, and international statistics. Nonetheless, it was believed that if one wanted the accurate up-to-date (as of the 1960s) figures for age, sex, marital status, nationality and racial groups, city–country, ancient civilizations, and so forth, Dublin's book was the place to go. It was the perfect source for a college term paper. Perhaps other people might have written a book of that sort, but perhaps not as elegantly. But Dublin was also a closet psychologist, as well as a close student of the social trends—and therein lies the book's unique strength and charm. Every student of the maladaptive aspects of the human condition should treat himself or herself to a good taste of the stock and broth contained within this meaty volume.

I thank Louis Dublin, the Grand Old Man of Suicidology, for this book because in it he has answered much of my cry for help and has given us all new clues to suicide.

SUICIDE

A Sociological and
Statistical Study

LOUIS I. DUBLIN

THE RONALD PRESS COMPANY   •   NEW YORK

[1986]

CONTENTS

SUICIDE: A SOCIOLOGICAL AND STATISTICAL STUDY

THE INFLUENCES OF WAR

Probably no mass activity of society exerts a deeper or more far-reaching influence on human conduct than war. Within the belligerent nations and the closely associated neutrals, every human activity which furthers the successful issue of the combat is forced to the limit and everything that does not aid the conflict is, for the time, neglected and discontinued. Contrary to what might be expected, times of reorganization and turmoil such as prevail during a war apparently do not increase that personal disintegration which leads to a larger number of self-inflicted deaths. It would seem that the all-engrossing, unaccustomed activities and the enlargement of interests to include more than the personal concerns of a limited circle of family and friends absorb people's entire attention and prevent them from morbid brooding over individual troubles and disappointments. In

From *Suicide: A Sociological and Statistical Study* (pp. 68–73), by L. I. Dublin, 1986, New York: Ronald Press Company. Reprinted with permission of the author's estate.

I picked this particular selection from Dublin's book because it touches on a huge topic—war—and the sociological interactions between war and suicide. Dublin wrote his book before distinctions were made between "good" and "bad" wars, and the corresponding impact on suicide rates.

wartime the State needs all the energy of its citizens. People feel wanted and needed and have no time to indulge in personal or imaginary worries.

During the years of the two World Wars, suicide rates fell, with few exceptions, and in general reached their lowest point toward the end of the periods. In the United States the suicide rate began to decline in 1941 and continued to drop until 1944. In World War I, the rate began to decline in 1916 and continued to drop until by 1920 it had reached the lowest point recorded since 1903.

In England and Wales, the rate dropped 25 per cent for males between 1938 and 1944, and 30 per cent for females. Much the same phenomenon occurred in the First World War, when the rate dropped 25 per cent between 1914 and 1918. Unfortunately, data are not available for Germany during World War II, but in the earlier one, the 1918 suicide rate was the lowest ever recorded for that country. In Austria the decline during World War II was more than 50 per cent for each sex. In both France and Italy the suicide rate dropped more than 40 per cent for males, and for females it was 44 per cent less in Italy, and 32 per cent less in France. In Japan the incidence of suicide decreased about 9 per cent during the First World War and 11 per cent for males during the Second.

Even in the non-belligerent countries similar declines took place in both World Wars. Neutral Sweden reported a decline of 18 per cent during the Second World War and more than 7 per cent in the First. Even in the Netherlands, which was seriously involved by the German occupation, the rate for men during World War II dropped 36 per cent.[1]

A study of pre-war and post-war suicide rates in most European countries shows that suicide became less prevalent from 1938 to 1944, paralleling the condition prevailing in World War I. There was a dip during the war, with a subsequent rise in the post-war period.

Records of the nineteenth century show similar fluctuations during war years. In this country, suicide declined during the Civil War, judging by the statistics of Massachusetts and Connecticut, two states with fairly reliable figures. In the years of 1856–1860 the suicide rate averaged 8.0 per 100,000 population in Massachusetts and 6.1 in Connecticut. During the war years 1861–1865, it fell to 6.3 and 4.6, respectively, in the two states. Abroad, during the general upheavals and revolutions of 1848 and 1849, suicides diminished throughout almost all Europe. During the Franco-Prussian War, France had 1,041 fewer suicides in 1870 and 708 fewer in 1871 than the four-year average recorded from 1866–1869. Germany and Austria witnessed similar reductions during those years.

One explanation of this phenomenon is that, of course, for men in the prime of life there were opportunities to get killed in battle—so there

---

[1] Peter Sainsbury, *The Social and Epidemiological Aspects of Suicide with Special Reference to the Aged.* (New York: Atherton Press, 1963).

56

was convenient a more honorable and satisfying method of death than committing suicide. "And for our country 'tis bliss to die." The psychiatrists remind us that in times of war aggressions which normally tend to be directed against one's self are more likely to be directed outward at the common enemy. Incidentally, though the decline in the rate is usually greater among men than among women, the latter, too, show a distinct reduction. In England and Wales, Scotland, the Irish Free State, and Finland, they showed a larger decline than the men in the World War II years. In some countries, on the other hand, the women showed a notable increase in suicide—for example, in Switzerland, where their rate increased 27 per cent between 1938 and 1944; in Denmark, 59 per cent; and Norway, 85 per cent. In both these Scandanavian countries, which were occupied by the Germans, the brunt of the war apparently bore down harder on women than on men.[2]

Even in Japan, with its traditionally high suicide rates, the same phenomenon appeared. For many years, the Japanese rate had centered around 20 per 100,000. In the five years preceding World War II, Japan was already engaged in an intensive war operation on the continent of Asia, and by 1940 the suicide rate had dropped to 13.8 per 100,000. By the close of the war in 1945, it was still only 15.3, but subsequently it rose to 19.9 in 1950 and 25.3 in 1955, at which level it has stabilized. This trend apparently has affected both the urban and rural population.

It should not be inferred that military service per se presupposes a low suicide rate among its participants. It does not. In the past, suicide has been frequent among soldiers in peacetime. Dr. Bernard D. Karpinos[3] of the Office of the Surgeon General of the U.S. Army, who has studied suicide in our armed forces over the long period 1910–1958, reports that the rate for enlisted men declined from a high point of more than 50 per 100,000 in 1915 and 1916 to lows of about 7 per 100,000 in 1945 and about 8 in 1946. The rates showed marked declines during the war years 1917 through 1919 and, more particularly, during 1941 through 1945. Officer personnel as a group have considerably higher rates than the enlisted men, but this difference is largely due to their higher average ages. They, too, showed marked declines during the years of both World Wars. On the average, during the long period covered by this study, the suicide rate of Army personnel has been higher than that of civilian males at comparable ages except under age 25. The suicide rate among white men in the Army is 38 per cent above that of Negroes.

Firearms, which are accessible, are the means employed in 62 per cent of the suicides of soldiers. Poisoning (mainly carbon monoxide gas) follows with 17 per cent; then hanging and strangulation, 14 per cent; and other

---

[2]*Ibid.*
[3]Bernard D. Karpinos, "Suicide among Military Personnel," unpublished data.

methods, 7 per cent. Dr. Karpinos points out that for all Army personnel the use of firearms and explosives tends to decrease with age; this method was used in 74 per cent of the suicides in the youngest age group. The use of poisoning, on the other hand, appears to gain prominence with age. Among the officers, 72 per cent used firearms, followed by poisoning, 18 per cent.

. . .

The findings summarized above are in agreement with those previously recorded by Durkheim in his classic study. He noted that in all European countries, the incidence of suicide among soldiers was much higher than in the civilian population. He believed that common soldiers, the majority of whom are not married and thus lack close family ties, are more likely than civilians to do away with themselves. On the other hand, officers, who frequently are married, showed even higher suicide rates. He thought that because of their training and environment members of the armed forces set little value on their lives. He further pointed out that the suicide rate increased among those who had been in the armed forces for the longest period of time, although one might assume that re-enlisted men, in particular, would have adjusted to conditions prevailing in the service. Karpinos reports the same findings in the American Army, but points out that the men with the longest period of service are also the more advanced in age and that this alone would account for their higher suicide rates. The atmosphere in which a solider and his officer live and their readiness to make sacrifices, Durkheim believed, helped us to understand why they are capable of self-destruction for even minor causes, such as reprimand, failure to get leave, or even because other suicides have occurred near them.

This study of the effect of wartime activity would indicate that a social movement great enough to unite large numbers of people in a common enthusiasm so intense as to leave little opportunity for introspection and worry about one's individual shortcomings, tends definitely to lower the suicide rate. Furthermore, war tremendously stimulates business activity and temporarily provides large numbers of people with additional employment, with increased income, and, perhaps even more important, with a sense of usefulness and personal worth. Of course, the aftermath of war ordinarily involves social disorder and economic chaos; and these conditions are reflected in great increases in suicide mortality. When we balance the lower wartime rates with the higher rates prevailing during post-war disorganization, it cannot be said with any assurance that war tends to lower the suicide rate over the long run.

5

IGA
THE THORN IN THE CHRYSANTHEMUM: SUICIDE AND ECONOMIC SUCCESS IN MODERN JAPAN

Originally published in Berkeley, 1986

Many people who live in civilized countries today are at least bilingual, but it is still a marvelous rarity to find an individual who is truly bicultural. A relatively new branch of neuropsychology is the study of the two hemispheres—or split brain—for which a Nobel prize was awarded recently. Professor Mamoru Iga is a bicultural man; his brain (metaphorically speaking) has Eastern and Western hemispheres, happily united under one figurative *corpus collosum*, whose separate images are completely fused and come to us, synthesized, in one unique view presented in straightforward prose.

In this book, Iga illuminates two sides of Japanese culture, not Ruth Benedict's well-known characterization of Japan in terms of the chyrsanthemum and the sword but rather in terms of two aspects of the chyrsanthemum itself. On the one hand, Iga discusses the positive aspects of the chyrsanthemum side of Japan, the aesthetic qualities, the high drive and ambition, the intense cultural cohesion, and the outstanding economic success of contemporary Japan. On the other hand, he points our attention to the canker, the worm, the thorn in the chrysanthemum. In all this, Iga implies that there is a quid pro quo, that there are specific aspects to the "price" of success. In this book he explicates one especially onerous aspect of that price—suicide.

In the 1960s, when I was doing a lecture tour on suicide in several cities in Japan—arranged in part by Iga—I was speaking in a great university hall. A student stood and asked me a question: Could I tell him why he should not, at his age, take his life in order to be at one with Nature? I mentally invoked Mill's Method of Difference and answered him by asking him to imagine that he was one of a set of identical twins, one of whom had committed suicide at his age, and the other of whom had survived to live 40 or 50 years, and whether at that future time the twin who had survived would be glad that he had done so. The student sat down, obviously totally unconvinced. Later, my Japanese host told me that my response had been a good answer, but unfortunately it had been a Western answer. What, I asked him, would I have to have done to have supplied a meaningful response? First of all, he said, I would had to have been born in Japan.

Iga was born in Japan—some 80 years ago. He lived his first 32 years in that country, attending school and university. He taught there. He was, in a word, Japanese. Then, through a complicated set of circumstances, he came to the United States, where he completed his education, acquired a PhD, and attended Harvard University for postdoctoral study. He married, raised a family, and had a distinguished career as a university professor. He tells me that he dreams and thinks in English but is also capable of thinking the Japanese way. And, even more important, he can put the two languages together.

There are enormous important differences in the styles of logic between Eastern and Western thinking. One cannot simply translate from Japanese into English as one would translate from, say, French or German into English. We must recognize that there are many logics other than the traditional Aristotelian logic of the Western world. The bridge from East to West has to traverse a rutted road between mentational styles as well as between different vocabularies and different alphabets. Hajime Nakamura's 1960 epic book on the Asiatic logics, *The Ways of Thinking of Eastern Peoples*, is indispensible here.

Iga's focus on the value of suicide notes is of special importance. In 1968, during one of his sojourns in Japan to study suicide, he made a special study of suicide notes. Translations of many of these appear in his volume, with great force and effectiveness. In many ways suicide notes provide a unique window into the heart and mind of the suicidal person, especially when these notes are put into the context of a specific life and culture.

Also noteworthy is Iga's emphasis on the lives (and deaths) of certain Japanese writers. It was fascinating for me to read his insightful accounts of Yukio Mishima and Yasunari Kawabata, especially after I had read several of their novels and a series of accounts of their deaths. But in reading the explanations here, I had the feeling that I was on the ground floor, yet reading in a language that I could understand.

Iga is most qualified to explain Japanese suicide to an American or Western readership. He understands suicide theory; he is a close student of Durkheim's works and knows about psychodynamic formulations. He is in position to tell us, as perhaps no one else is, about suicide in Japan in terms that we can understand. He is reporting about a culture that he knows. He is not doing field work; he is performing homework. He has an inborn understanding of his native country, of its ancient history, of its recent past, of its present, of its future, that no American missionary, no university anthropologist, no visiting scholar could ever hope to attain. And, fortunately for us, he has the wish and the gift to share it all with us in the language through which he now thinks. In my mind, he is the most eminent American-Japanese suicidologist in the world. On this topic, he speaks *ex templa*.

Today, Japan is our giant friendly competitor, our rivalous sibling in the economic world scene. In this sense, every sophisticated American will want to read this book to gain additional insights into the mind of the new "big kid on the block." And every suicidologist should read this book for at least two reasons: To widen one's appreciation of the cultural aspects of suicide and to deepen one's understanding of suicide as a ubiquitous phenomenon and of the ubiquitous features of suicide itself.

THE THORN
IN THE
CHRYSANTHEMUM

SUICIDE AND
ECONOMIC SUCCESS
IN MODERN JAPAN

MAMORU IGA

Forewords by
Edwin S. Shneidman
and
David K. Reynolds

UNIVERSITY OF CALIFORNIA PRESS
Berkeley • Los Angeles • London
[1986]

CONTENTS

THE THORN IN THE CHRYSANTHEMUM

JAPANESE VALUE ORIENTATIONS

The discussions of suicide among Japanese youths, women, and writers showed the importance of social structure in relation to suicide. The concept of anomic suicide (as indicated by a wide discrepancy between ego ideal and self-conception, the sense of relative deprivation, greed, disillusionment, and jealousy) facilitates the understanding of college-student suicides. Because of the high emphasis on education and ambition, the importance of a wide disparity between goals and means as a cause of suicide also applies generally to Japanese youths.

A UNESCO study by Jean Stoetzel in 1951–52 found Japanese youths to be highly ambitious, hankering after fame, but unable to give any details about how to attain their goals. The Japanese youth was very self-confident, but his self-confidence was based on "faith in his star, not

From *The Thorn in the Chrysanthemum: Suicide and Economic Success in Modern Japan* (pp. 114–138), by M. Iga, 1986, Berkeley: University of California Press. Copyright 1986 The Regents of the University of California. Reprinted with permission.

I picked this particular selection from Iga's book because it illustrates how an anthropological study of an unfamiliar culture (Japan) can focus on quasi-psychological factors such as ambition, status, groupism, conformity. It is a kind of oriental Durkheim, with a more iconoclastic twist. I knew Mamoru Iga well, and I like to hear his voice in his text.

belief in his present judgment, will-power, and efficiency." His personality was characterized by high ambivalence, ambiguity, passivity and resignation, lack of imagination, insecurity, and escapism. These characteristics also appear to be important elements of the Japanese youth's personality today.

Many Japanese women's suicides were fatalistic, due to sex prejudice, with resulting resentment, fear, and resignation. Some others were of the anomic type, due to role conflicts that produced a wide goal-means discrepancy and disillusionment. Writers' suicides are difficult to categorize because they appear more various in motivation. Arishima's suicide seems to show more elements of egoistic suicide (e.g., a desire to find meaning in life), Akutagawa's suicide shows elements of fatalistic suicide (e.g., his strong sense of family obligation, resentment, and resignation), and Dazai's suicide shows elements of anomic suicide (e.g., his inflated ego ideal and dependency). Mishima's suicide may be categorized as an altruistic one, at least on his conscious level, because it was a demonstration against the "corrupt" Japan of the postwar period. He showed a high degree of integration into Japanese tradition. Kawabata's suicide was egoistic, because he was a self-sufficient thinker. In his case, physical illness seems to have been the most important factor. (If there is a rational suicide—that is, suicide as a result of thorough contemplation of all alternatives—Kawabata's suicide appears to have come close to it.) However, on a deeper level, the suicides of all these writers may be attributed to the discrepancy between their ego ideal and self-concept (for example, losing creativity).

Suicide is mostly caused by a failure to attain personal goals because of inadequate means. Inadequate means include "inimical" behavior, illness, declining creativity, and weak ego. Weak ego is characterized by a strong dependency need, a tendency toward emotionalism, high susceptibility to group pressure, a lack of reality testing, and weak impulse control.

Some of the data used in these discussions were from studies done in the mid-1950s, when Japanese suicide rates were highest (in 1958, 25.7 per 100,000: 30.7 for males and 20.8 for females). However, as Christopher observed in 1982, feudalistic remnants of behavior patterns—such as education characterized by memorization, a strong stress on power and status difference, and sex and ethnic prejudices—are still prevalent in present-day Japan. Compared with the 1950s, there is even a sign of the strong revival of traditionalism in the 1980s, with the decline in prestige of their model—American democracy. The revival is marked by the governmental control of Japanese education.

Discussed in this chapter are the components of Japanese social structure that largely determine the goal-means discrepancy—that is, the value orientations that produce unrealistically high aspirations and inadequate means to achieve them.

At the risk of oversimplification, table 32 describes Japanese culture

TABLE 32
A Comparison of Japanese and American Value Orientations

Problem of Life	Japanese	American[1]
1. Man-Nature relationship	Monism Polytheism Mysticism	Dualism Monotheism Rationalism
2. Valued personality type	Groupism	Individualism
Emphasis on:	Harmony Selflessness Competition for group goals	Ego-strength Self-assertion Competition for self-interest
3. Time orientation	Accommodationism "Field dependent" Short-time perspective	"Field independent" Future orientation
Emphasis on:	Adjustment	Development, change
View of future:	Insecurity about future	Optimism about future
4. Mode of social relations	Familism Authoritarianism	Mechanistic view of society Egalitarianism
Emphasis on:	Faith, loyalty	Efficiency, cleanliness, orderliness
Values counterbalancing individualism for social integration		Love, fair play, cooperation, conscience, group sport, humanitarianism

[1] Adapted from John Gillin, "National and Regional Cultural Values in the United States," *Social Forces* 34 (December 1955): 107–113.

in comparison with American culture. The American material has been adapted from John Gillin's characterization of American culture. The comparison is made of the basic problems that all peoples have to solve: the Man-Nature relationship, the valued personality type, time orientation, and the mode of social relations.

The American view of the Man-Nature relationship is dualistic: man versus nonhuman, including Nature and God. The separation of man from Nature promotes rationalism; eventually, everything, including God, has become the object of reasoning. At the same time, an ideal is separate from natural phenomena—that is, the law ("what ought to be") versus existence ("what is").

The valued personality type among Americans is individualistic, with emphasis on self-interest, self-development, and self-reliance. The modality of social relations is revealed in principles for social integration and collateral values. The American view of social integration is mechanistic, holding that society is like a machine. It operates well only when its parts are clean, efficient, and coordinated in an orderly fashion. Hence, values of cleanliness, efficiency, and orderliness are expected. Since "efficient" Americans use reasoning for attaining self-profit, their social integration requires values that counterbalance self-profit—for example, Americans place strong emphasis on love, cooperation, conscience, fair play, humanitarian assistance, and group sport. The American culture is also characterized by future orientation. It aims at future success and development. Because of American faith in development, together with the historical experience of their frontier, Americans are optimistic about life and change.

In comparison, Japanese culture is characterized by monism, groupism, familism, and accommodationism, as explained on the following pages. Of course, these are persisting elements of Japanese tradition. The more traditional are Japanese persons, the more strongly they manifest these traits. These elements of Japanese tradition are quite applicable to explanations of Japanese behavior patterns, whether of suicide or of economic success.

III

BIOLOGICAL INSIGHTS

6

STOFF AND MANN
THE NEUROBIOLOGY OF SUICIDE:
FROM THE BENCH TO THE CLINIC

Originally published in New York, 1997

My mentor, Henry Murray—physician and personologist—reminded me that human behavior has a biological home: "No brain, no mind." The entire biochemical and biological approach to all of psychology and psychiatry points to the *biological* investigations of suicidal phenomena. In addition to 19th-century sociological and psychological avenues of approach, there is the "scientific" thread, that is, the biological ways of using family histories (genetical), the microscopic assay of central nervous system tissue, and the laboratory analysis of central nervous system fluids.

Curiously enough, there is, to date, no single authored book of note on this vast topic. There are hundreds of published articles in the learned journals and a number of important edited volumes, some quite recent. In this special list there is *Suicide*, edited by Alec Roy, an English-trained psychiatrist working in the United States. His contributors include Marie Åsberg of Sweden; Keith Hawton and Peter Sainsbury of Great Britain; Norman Kreitman of Scotland; F. A. Whitlock of Australia; and Seymour Kety, George Murphy, and Eli Robins of the United States. The topics cover genetics, biochemistry, alcoholism, and schizophrenia. The publication date of Roy's book is 1986.

The Biology of Suicide, also published in 1986, was edited by Ronald Maris, an eminent American sociologist. His contributors, mostly American, include Frederick Goodwin, Jerome Motto, and Alec Roy. The topics of biological correlates of suicide, genetics, alcoholism, endocrinology, and encephalography are discussed.

There is a 1997 volume with a decided European slant, published in The Netherlands by Greek editors. It is *Suicide: Biopsychosocial Approaches*, and the principal editor is Alexander J. Botsis, who is the psychiatrist-in-chief of the Hellenic Army Medical Corps. The 24 chapters are subsumed under four parts: Epidemiology, Etiopathegenetic Considerations, Clinical Issues, and Conceptual and Ethical Issues. The contributors in common with the other two books are few: Alec Roy and Herman van Praag. Again, there are chapters on mood disorders and schizophrenia, heredity, and violence. The book is based on a selection of papers presented at the meeting of the International Association of Suicide Prevention in Athens in 1996. To my ears it has an interesting but somewhat exotic sound and has some derivative echoes of papers given at an exhibition.

The best summary I know on this topic is a chapter entitled "The Biology of Suicide" by Morton Silverman, of the University of Chicago, in yet another edited book, *Comprehensive Textbook of Suicidology and Suicide Prevention*, compiled by Ronald Maris, Alan Berman, and Morton Silverman and published by Guilford Press in 1999.

The most recent and comprehensive book on this subject is *The Neurobiology of Suicide: From the Bench to the Clinic*, published by the New York Academy of Sciences in 1997. The editors are David M. Stoff and John J. Mann of the National Institute of Mental Health and the New York State Psychiatric Institute, respectively. They declare that their volume describes the most promising research findings over the past decade on suicide research.

Some of the findings, especially in genetical studies and biochemical assays, are enormously suggestive. I have puzzled as to why they trouble me, and I shall attempt to set down here some of my thoughts on this. I must begin by saying that almost every one of the primary authors in this field has voiced his or her own cautions, so that these thoughts are not solely my own and are really not iconoclastic, in that they echo the caveats of the saints who produced the original miracles. I list my concerns, briefly,

1. That what is being measured (with such precision) is general *perturbation*, and not specifically suicide. Of course, "being upset" is related to changes in body func-

tioning. But here is the first (of 17) "major research findings" about the biology of suicide from the Preface of one of edited books (cited above): "Low levels (e.g., below 92.5 nmol/liter) of hydroxyindoleacetic acid (5-HIAA; a metabolite of the neurotransmitter serotonin, or 5=HT) in cerebrospinal fluid (CSF) is predictive of suicidal acts, especially violent suicides" (p. vii). *Predictive* of suicide?

2. That what is being measured is *concomitant*, and not *causative*. If one (unethically) effected low levels of 5-HIAA in prisoners, would they then automatically commit suicide? These biochemical values reflect inner physiological states; they are not necessarily precursors of specific behaviors. They seem certainly to coexist; they do not necessarily preexist.

3. That physiological values are being related to syndromes that are *peripheral* to suicide—schizophrenia and alcoholism—and to depression, which may or may not be isomorphic with suicide. Converting suicide into depression is a kind of methodological sleight of hand. The central fact about depression is that one can lead a long, unhappy life with depression; indeed, it is not a legitimate cause of a death entry on a death certificate; whereas the whole point of suicide prevention is to *prevent* a death. Suicide and depression are not synonymous. Converting the study of suicide into the study of depression is like moving the lamplight to the votes that you want counted.

4. That the biologizing of suicide is an integral part of the medicalization of what is essentially—so I believe—a phenomenological decision of the mind. I am a radical mentalist. I believe that the mind has a mind of its own; that the main business of the mind is to mind its own business. I believe that a discipline can only be as scientific as its basic subject matter will allow, and I am on the lookout for specious accuracy when it gives itself the mantle of Trust.

I include this selection on the biology of suicide because this topic cannot be left out and because I wanted to take advantage of the arena that I have created in which to voice my minority view.

In my own mind I am not damning with faint praise when I say that the book by Stoff and Mann is the best on the biology of suicide. What is true is my belief that the reductionistic biological analyses do not provide the lubricating fluids for the essences of suicide. In the last analysis, I do not think that the key answers about suicide are to be found in the brain; I think that the key action is in the mind. But were I the head of the National Institute of Mental Health national program on the study of suicide and its prevention—as I once was —I would certainly support and fund research on the biological aspects of suicide—as I once did.

ANNALS OF THE NEW YORK ACADEMY OF SCIENCES
Volume 836

THE NEUROBIOLOGY OF SUICIDE

FROM THE BENCH TO THE CLINIC

Edited by David M. Stoff and J. John Mann

The New York Academy of Sciences
New York, New York
[1997]

CONTENTS

ANNALS OF THE NEW YORK ACADEMY OF SCIENCES

Volume 836
December 29, 1997

THE NEUROBIOLOGY OF SUICIDE FROM THE BENCH TO THE CLINIC[a]

Editors and Conference Organizers
DAVID M. STOFF and J. JOHN MANN

[a]This volume is the result of a conference, entitled **Suicide Research Workshop: From the Bench to the Clinic**, held in Washington, D.C. on November 14–15, 1996, by the National Institute of Mental Health and the American Suicide Foundation.

THE NEUROBIOLOGY OF SUICIDE: FROM THE BENCH TO THE CLINIC

SUICIDE RESEARCH: OVERVIEW AND INTRODUCTION

Modern Suicide Research

Today, suicide is one of the most significant public health threats in the United States. In 1994 suicide was the ninth leading cause of death in the United States (among the general population). It claims more than 30,000 lives each year and is the third leading cause of death among young people aged 15–24 years. The costs and consequences of suicide in the United States are far-reaching and devastating, both financially and socially. It is the sixth leading cause of years and years of potential life lost before the age of 65. To respond to this major public health problem, we must increase systematic research efforts to identify high-risk groups, understand etiology, and develop effective treatment and prevention strategies. In the past, most research on suicide risk has focused on the role of

From "The Neurobiology of Suicide: From the Bench to the Clinic," by D. M. Stoff & J. J. Mann, 1997. New York: *Annals of the New York Academy of Sciences*, 836, pp. 1, 5–11. Copyright 1997 by the New York Academy of Sciences. Reprinted with permission.
I picked this particular selection from Stoff and Mann's book simply because, as the overview of their edited volume, it is easily the most appropriate single piece to represent their entire enterprise.

psychological and sociocultural factors that are clearly important in determining risk. However, efforts aimed at identifying the potentially suicidal individual using demographic, social, developmental and psychological factors offer too weak a prediction to be of substantial clinical utility. It is believed that a biological perspective, which has grown out of the expanding research on the biochemical bases of mood disorders, is a promising approach to suicide research. It can assist in the investigation of risk factors that predispose a person to suicidal behavior and that increase understanding of etiology, treatment, and, ultimately, prevention. . . .

CLINICAL NEUROSCIENCE RESEARCH

It is hoped that understanding the neuroscientific substrates of suicidal behavior will lead to increased predictability in at-risk individuals, better diagnosis, and the development of more effective treatment and prevention strategies. In essence, the major task is to provide a road map of brain functioning and neurochemistry correlated with suicidal behavior, taking advantage of the powerful modern methods of molecular biology, quantitative morphometrics, and neurochemistry. Additional impetus for the neurobiological study of suicide comes from the implications of a genetic contribution to the risk for suicidal acts (Roy et al., this volume).

The two main strategies used to study the neurobiology of suicide are neuroendocrine challenges (e.g., HPA axis) and neurotransmitter (e.g., serotonin) measures. Neuroendocrine systems have not been as intensively investigated as the neurotransmitter systems. Nevertheless, neuroendocrine studies are noteworthy in representing some of the initial endeavors to identify biological correlates of suicide.

The earliest report of a biological abnormality derives from the observation of metabolic abnormalities and adrenocortical dysfunction in a seriously suicidal patient with Cushing's syndrome (among whom emotional and mental disturbances are frequent).[22] Subsequent reports in Cushing's syndrome also suggested endocrine abnormalities in suicide. For example, a female patient with a mental disorder accompanying Cushing's syndrome experienced a remission of suicidal ideation and risk after receiving deep X-ray therapy to the pituitary gland.[23] More recently, a study of 35 individuals with Cushing's syndrome revealed that six (17%) patients had recurrent suicidal thoughts, and two (7%) of these had made suicide attempts since the onset of their hypercortisolism.[24] Although endocrine profiles with ACTH and urinary-free cortisol are not presented for patients with suicidal ideation or suicide attempts, those with the most severe depressive clinical presentations had persistently and significantly elevated ACTH levels.[24] These data support the hypothesis that suicidal behavior, at least in a subgroup of patients with hypercortisolism, may be associated with dysregulation of the hypothalamic-pituitary-adrenal (HPA) axis.

The possibility that hyperactivity of the HPA axis might have a special relationship to suicidal behavior was initially suggested by investigators of the National Institute of Mental Health who observed elevated urinary 17-hydroxycorticosteroids, an indirect measure of daily cortisol production, in patients who later committed suicide.[25,26] However, several subsequent studies investigating this association have yielded mixed results.[27-29] In addition, investigations of relationships between suicidal behavior and plasma cortisol levels, before and after administration of dexamethasone, have also yielded contradictory results. Most studies found higher rates of nonsuppression on the dexamethasone suppression test (DST) in patients who had attempted or completed suicide compared to nonsuicide attempters.[30-33] There are, however, some negative studies reporting no association of recent suicidal behavior and nonsuppression of DST.[34,35] More recently, suicide victims have been found to have reduced binding of corticotropin-releasing factor (CRF) in the frontal cortex.[36] Inasmuch as it is thought that CRF hypersecretion is the basis of cortisol dysregulation in depression, this finding is consistent with the hypothesis that CRF is hypersecreted in depression with resulting receptor downregulation.

The majority of clinical neurobiological studies of suicide have concentrated on the serotonin (5-HT) system. A rationale for the intensive study of 5-HT is that it occupies a key role in other-directed aggression and impulsivity as well as a variety of other physiologic and behavioral functions of animals. The link between other-directed aggression/impulsivity and inner-directed aggression (i.e., self-destructive and suicidal behavior) has been frequently commented upon. Serotonergic function bears a similar relationship to aggression in animal models of aggression[37] and clinical studies of suicide and aggression. Although remarkable progress has been made in clarifying the role of the serotonin (5-HT) system in suicide, the basic neurobiology of suicide risk has yet to be elucidated, and a distinct and complete constellation of neurochemical/neuroanatomical deficits in suicide has yet to be identified.

Most 5-HT studies of suicide attempters have demonstrated abnormalities in related 5-HT indices, leading to the hypothesis that reduced serotonergic activity is associated with increased suicide risk (see review by Mann[38]). The first study of the relationship between 5-HT function and attempted suicide comes from a cerebrospinal fluid (CSF) study of 5-hydroxyindoleacetic acid (5-HIAA), the principal metabolite of 5-HT, in depressive illness.[39,40] The finding that CSF 5-HIAA concentration was bimodally distributed in depressed patients generated interest in discovering clinical correlates of the two modes of the CSF 5-HIAA distribution (Åsberg, this volume). It was noted that a history of serious suicide attempts was associated with low CSF 5-HIAA concentration, in particular, when violent methods were employed. It has been pointed out that the failure to show uniformly low 5-HT function in studies of suicide attempters may be due to the complexity of attempted suicide and the difficulties in controlling and assessing numerous variables in behaving subjects. Studies of 5-HT turnover in suicide attempters have also employed the platelet serotonin transporter, and 5-HT$_{2A}$ receptor and neuroendocrine strategies (Pandey, this volume). Alterations in the serotonergic system in the brain of suicide victims also supports the hypothesis that reduced serotonergic activity is associated with increased suicide risk (see review by Mann et al.[41]). The first neurochemical studies of suicide completers involved the measurement of monoamines and their metabolites in brain tissue. Similar to the majority of studies showing low CSF 5-HIAA in attempters, brain stem levels of 5-HT and 5-HIAA are also reduced in most studies of suicide victims. Paralleling the CSF 5-HIAA findings in attempters, this reduction in brain stem 5-HT and in 5-HIAA is independent of psychiatric diagnosis, occurring in suicide attempters in several diagnostic groups (major depression, schizophrenia, personality disorders, and alcoholism). Postmortem brain stem measurements of 5-HT and 5-HIAA are difficult to interpret because of lack of stability after death, anatomical heterogeneity, and uncertainty about the mechanisms (synthesis, transport, catabolism) accounting for brain levels. Investigators have therefore turned their attention to measurement of postsynaptic receptors or transporter sites in discrete brain regions of suicide victims [Kleinman (Bachus et al.), Stockmeier, Ordway, Rajkowska, and Arango et al., this volume]. These postmortem studies will provide the necessary information for the eventual application to *in vivo* imaging studies in suicide attempters and at-risk individuals.

CLINICAL THERAPEUTICS

The earliest treatment approaches to suicide were based on the dominant views of the origin and causes of suicide rather than strict empirical evidence. These views are embodied in sociologic, psychologic, and psychosocial theories, and with minor modifications they could also be generalized to other forms of psychopathology. The sociological treatment approach targets the individual's response to the social milieu. One of the earliest psychological treatment approaches had a psychodynamic emphasis concentrating on intrapsychic conflicts where suicide is "aggression turned inward." Other psychotherapeutic approaches have enlarged the possible internal dynamics that predispose to suicide and have also addressed an interpersonal component. The psychosocial treatment approach recognizes the importance of the individual and the social milieu, and emphasizes inner conflict as well as situational stresses, such as physical illness or disturbed interpersonal relations. Treatment interventions derived from these views have been limited in their effectiveness and do not seem to be very helpful in the prevention of suicide.

More modern strategies for the treatment of suicide come from the psychiatric, neurobiologic/clinical psychopharmacological and cognitive-behavioral fields (see Fawcett et al., Linehan, Montgomery, and Tondo et al., this volume). The ideal focus should be primary prevention, and interventions should be multidisciplinary. Treatment of suicidal patients is based on an understanding of the risk factors for suicide, a set of general management principles for suicidal patients, and the treatment of the associated psychiatric disorder. Specific treatment is directed at the underlying psychiatric disorder responsible for suicidal symptomatology. With the explosion of knowledge on the neurobiologic substrates underlying psychopathology, a neurobiological perspective can improve identification of suicidal persons and hence offers promise for new prevention strategies. The development of more novel pharmacotherapeutic approaches for suicidal patients depends, at least in part, on advances in clinical neuroscience to determine the neurobiological mechanisms underlying the threshold for suicidal behavior. Based on neurobiological abnormalities, there may be a suicidal subgroup of patients with a serotonergic deficiency in whom serotonergic enhancement may be most beneficial. Preclinical basic research models relevant to suicide may one day also inform treatment research to the extent that they assist in uncovering mechanisms underlying suicide.

In the past decade, increasing attention has been paid to cognitive factors that may contribute to suicidal behavior. The impetus for examining the role of cognitive processing in suicide has come largely from the paradigm shift in behavior therapy to the cognitive domain and, indirectly, from research on cognitive aspects of depression and suicide. Cognitive therapy, developed as a result of empirical investigations with depressed patients, has received attention because of its demonstrated efficacy in the treatment of unipolar depression. Beck and colleagues[42] have shown an association of hopelessness and impaired problem solving in suicidal patients that may have been sensitive to cognitive therapy.

One caveat that must be kept in mind is that there is no single reason why individuals commit suicide, and suicide is the outcome of multiple influences that bear on it. Therefore, a single treatment approach may be effective often, but sometimes a combination of treatments that matches the individual needs to be employed. Additionally, other avenues of study are also relevant to suicide treatment research. In the future, designing treatments for the specific susceptibility to suicidal acts, apart from the associated psychiatric illness, may represent an important approach. There has been some interest in ameliorating the conditions that theoretically would predispose an individual to suicidal behavior by attempting to reduce suicidal ideation. In a similar way, it would be useful to design treatment modalities that might specifically address how to reduce impulsive-aggressive behavior and other high-risk personality traits. Drug development research aimed at the design of specific antisuicidal agents is similar to the strategy of developing "serenics," a new category of specific antiaggressive drugs based on 5-HT agonist activity.

By and large, there has been little progress in the development of effective treatments for suicidal behavior, at least relative to the advances that have occurred in the therapeutics of mood disorders and other major psychiatric disorders. This is due, at least in part, to the belief that it is ethically unsound to include a suicidal patient in a randomized trial that might require withholding treatment. The consequence associated with this practice of excluding suicidal patients from clinical treatment trials is a lack of data on this group and is discussed elsewhere in this volume (Linehan). Another factor that has hindered suicide treatment research is the absence of a sensitive and specific predictor of suicide that allows identification of a high-risk group. This state of affairs represents a strong rationale for many of the neurobiological studies presented in greater detail in this volume.

An important theme underlying current suicide research is that suicide risk factors are drawn from multiple domains (demographic, social, psychological, developmental, psychiatric, genetic, and biologic) demanding a multidisciplinary approach for their study. Close collaboration of basic and clinical scientists is required for the development of the most promising preclinical models to guide clinical investigations, identification of specific neurobiologic abnormalities in suicidal patients, and the translation of these findings into clinically useful applications.

REFERENCES

...

22. TRETHOWAN, W. H. & S. COBB. 1952. Neuropsychiatric aspects of Cushing's syndrome. AMA Arch. Neurol. Psychiatry **67:** 283–309.

23. SPILLANE, J. 1954. Nervous and mental disorders in Cushing's syndrome. Brain **74:** 72–93.

24. STARKMAN, M. N., D. E. SCHTEINGART & M. A. SHORK. 1981. Depressed mood and other psychiatric manifestations of Cushing's syndrome: Relationship to hormone levels. Psychosom. Med. **43:** 3–18.

25. BUNNEY, W. E., JR. & J. A. FAWCETT. 1965. Possibility of a biochemical test for suicide potential. Arch. Gen. Psychiatry **13:** 232–239.

26. BUNNEY, W. E., JR., J. A. FAWCETT, J. M. DAVIS & S. GIFFORD. 1969. Further evaluation of urinary 17-hydroxycorticosteroids in suicidal patients. Arch. Gen. Psychiat. **21:** 138–150.

27. KRIEGER, G. 1974. The plasma level of cortisol as a predictor of suicide. Dis. Nerv. Syst. **35:** 237–240.

28. LEVY, G. & E. HANSEN. 1969. Failure of the urinary test for suicide potential. Arch. Gen. Psychiatry **20:** 415–418.

29. TRÄSKMAN, L., G. TYBRING, M. ÅSBERG, et al. 1980. Cortisol in the CSF of depressed and suicidal patients. Arch. Gen. Psychiatry **37:** 761–767.

30. CARROLL, B. J., J. F. GREDEN & M. FEINBERG. 1981. Suicide, neuroendocrine dysfunction and CSF 5-HIAA concentrations in depression. *In* Recent Advances in Neuropsychopharmacology. B. Angrist, Ed.: 307–313. Pergamon Press. Oxford and New York.

31. CORYELL, W. & M. A. SCHLESSER. 1981. Suicide and the dexamethasone suppression test in unipolar depression. Am. J. Psychiatry **138:** 1120–1121.

32. TARGU, S. D., L. ROSEN & A. E. CAPODANNO. 1981. The dexamethasone suppression test in suicidal patients with unipolar depression. Am J. Psychiatry **140:** 877–879.

33. BANKI, C. M. & M. ARATO. 1983. Amine metabolites and neuroendocrine response related to depression and suicide. J. Affective Disord. **5:** 223–232.

34. KOSCIS, J. H., S. KENNEDY, R. P. BROWN, J. J. MANN & B. MASON. 1986. Neuroendocrine studies in depression: Relationship to suicidal behavior. Ann. N.Y. Acad. Sci. **487:** 256–262.

35. VAN WETTERE, J. P., G. CHARLES & J. WILMOTTE. 1983. Test de function a la dexamethasone et suicide. Acta Psychiatr. Belg. **83:** 569–578.

36. NEMEROFF, C. B., M. J. OWENS, G. BISSETTE, A. C. ANDORN & M. STANLEY. 1988. Reduced corticotropin releasing factor binding sites in the frontal cortex of suicide victims. Arch. Gen. Psychiatry **45:** 577–579.

37. SOUBRIE, P. 1986. Reconciling the role of central serotonin neurons in human and animal behavior. Behav. Brain Sci. **9:** 319–364.

38. MANN, J. J. 1995. Violence and aggression. *In* Psychopharmacology: The Fourth Generation of Progress. D. J. Kupfer & Bloom, Eds.: 1919–1928. Raven Press. New York.

39. ASBERG, M., L. TRASKMAN & P. THOREN. 1976. 5-HIAA in the cerebrospinal fluid—a biochemical suicide predictor? Arch. Gen. Psychiatry **33:** 1119–1197.

40. ASBERG, M., L. THOREN, L. TRASKMAN, L. BERTILSSON & V. RINGBERGER. 1976. "Serotonin depression"—a biochemical subgroup within the affective disorders? Science **191:** 478–490.

41. MANN, J. J., M. D. UNDERWOOD & V. ARANGO. 1996. Postmortem studies of suicide victims. *In* Biology of Schizophrenia and Affective Disorders. S. J. Watson, Ed.: 197–221. American Psychiatric Press. Washington, D.C.

42. BECK, A. T., R. A. STEER & G. BROWN. 1993. Dysfunctional attitudes and suicidal ideation in psychiatric outpatients. Suicide Life Threatening Behav. **23:** 11–20.

IV

PSYCHIATRIC AND PSYCHOLOGICAL INSIGHTS

7

MENNINGER
MAN AGAINST HIMSELF

Originally published in New York, 1938

Freud's two best salesmen in America were Benjamin Spock (whose book *Baby and Child Care* sold more copies than any other book except the *Bible*) and Karl A. Menninger, America's avuncular all-American Kansas family psychiatrist. In a way, both men were baby doctors: Spock was the trustworthy pediatrician—it was said that all one needed to raise a child was a baby and a copy of Spock—and Menninger, who explained to America how childhood complexes could bedevil adult lives and introduced to and fostered America's acceptance of the habit of thinking in psychodynamic terms.

Man Against Himself begins felicitously—on the cover. The very name of the author, Karl A. Menninger, M.D., promises reliable advice and comfort for the soul (as we might expect from a country family doctor), and the well-chosen title is filled with intellectual implications. "Man against himself" implies at least the following: that an individual can be his or her own worst enemy; that we initiate behaviors that are inimical to our own best interests; that there is a range of these inimical behaviors, from saying the wrong thing to your

Adapted from a review, by E. S. Shneidman, 1998, *Contemporary Psychology*, 43, 461–464. Adapted with permission.

boss all the way to cutting your own throat; that important behaviors can be unconsciously motivated; that there is an effective unconscious component in human conduct; that here is a book on self-destruction, suicide, that is not sociologically centered; that the locus of the suicidal drama is in the mind of the individual, and most probably in the unconscious mind of the individual.

Man Against Himself, a 1930s book, is filled with enthusiasm and an urgency to do good. Seventy years later, it is regrettably accurate to say that many of the Freudian orthodoxies in the book are realistically beyond defense and that there may not be many provable statements in the book. Nonetheless, it stands as a marvelous, simply written book, filled with the sound of common sense. It is a landmark volume that has had enormous impact in thousands of American homes.

The book showed that Vienna, when translated in Topeka, played very well in Peoria. Peoria—and all of America—trusted that tall, impressive, homespun doctor from Kansas, who peppered his book with quotations from newspapers from all over the United States. Some readers thought that Menninger had made up the notion about the unconscious in Kansas, which gave those seductive ideas *bona fides* enough for any good American mother. By 1938, many New York psychoanalysts were already fugitives from Hitler, but certainly Menninger was not of this group. He was as American as apple pie and mothers, especially as American as mother's unconscious influences on her defenseless sons. Menninger also knew the ancient Greek stories about mothers and sons, but he pretty much kept this information to himself.

At the National Institute of Mental Health in the 1960s and on subsequent visits, it appeared to me that it was a fact of political life in the United States that mental health issues (like suicide) are viewed differently (and fare differently) under the two political parties. If it is true that knowledge follows funding, then the ways in which suicide is conceptualized and how it is treated depends somewhat on the political *zeitgeist* in Washington.

In this sense, *Man Against Himself* reflected the intellectual climate of the 1930s and of the New Deal and its relative openness to psychological thinking. Menninger's book was a brilliant psychiatric explication of the behind-the-scenes (i.e., unconscious) mental tensions of suicide, written, for the most part, in ordinary, everyday common language, and at the same time, it was a subtle political statement pointing toward an emphasis on "the human mind"—the title of another Menninger book.

Man Against Himself is not scholarly like Louis Dublin's sociologically oriented book *Suicide*; it is pleasantly anecdotal and wildly theoretical—Menninger has the undiluted courage of his own conceptions. But having said all this, I believe that *Man Against Himself* was by far the most important book on suicide written by an American and by far the most accessible.

As I see it, Menninger's basic hypothesis runs something like this: His major premise is that the universe is surfeited by conflict—hate, destruction, war, people expending time and energy to shorten and truncate their own lives—in short, a constricting and destructive force, a death instinct, the inimical tendencies within the personality. The second, minor premise addresses the question of why all of us do not commit suicide. The answer lies in the growth of inner personal strengths and defenses against our own libidinous (and destructive) urges, stronger in some of us than in others. The conclusion of this buried syllogistic reasoning is that in those cases in which suicide does occur we need to look to manifestations of the death instinct and the elaborations of the ubiquitous self-destructive tendencies. "Unconscious purposes are of more significance in understanding suicide than apparently simple, inevitable, external circumstances" (p. 19). In this book, Menninger sets himself the task of explicating the major unconscious psychological aspects of the omnipresent dark side of man.

> In all these the self-destructive urge is implicit or explicit. Seen thus it arrests our attention and demands that we scrutinize analytically these various ways in which men commit suicide, sometimes without knowing it. Such an analytic study I have essayed. (p. 8)

The main body of the book can be divided into two distinct parts, each congested with its own set of humming ideas. The first 80-some pages have to do with Menninger's original conceptualization of the deeper psychological motives for overt suicide, his dissection of the components of the death instinct; the remaining 380 pages are devoted to Menninger's discussions of various kinds of malignant self-destruction, subsuicide, partial suicide, substitutes for suicide, and subintentioned deaths—what Menninger calls *chronic, focal,* and *organic* suicides.

In 1910 there was a meeting on the topic of suicide in Freud's apartment in Vienna. On that occasion, Wilhelm Stekel, a psychoanalyst, pronounced that no one kills himself except one who wishes the death of another; that the suicidal person puts a dagger into his own chest to pierce the heart of the (ambivalently viewed) introjected love object, the father. Suicide is hostility. Stekel's notion was a psychodynamic formulation that caught on and was treated as gospel by generations of psychoanalytically oriented practitioners. Suicide was seen as murder in the 180th degree. Menninger wanted to improve on this idea, without rejecting the dramatic core of it.

In *Man Against Himself*, Menninger proposed that in each suicidal act there are three basic motives: (a) the wish to kill, (b) the wish to be killed, and (c) the wish to die. Menninger proposes all this *ex cathedra*: Eros and Thanatos; psychological anabolism and catabolism; life-enhancing and death-facilitating impulses. These make up the yin and yang of life. The three thanatological wishes now make sense, given the thanatological premise on which they rest.

Menninger feels that the wish to kill in suicide should be self-evident: "First of all suicide is obviously a *murder*. In the German language, it is, literally, a murder of the self (*Selbstmord*), and in all the earlier philosophic equivalents the idea of murder is implicit" (p. 4). It is a murder of the introjected love–hate figure.

> Suicide must thus be regarded as a peculiar kind of death which entails three basic internal elements and many modifying ones. There is the element of dying, the element of killing, and the element of being killed. Each is a condensation for which there exist complexes of motive, conscious and unconscious. What we call a suicide is for the individual himself an attempt to burst into life or to save his life. It may be to avoid something far more dreadful, to avoid committing murder or going mad. (p. 5)

If suicide, Menninger reasons, is a substitute for even more dreadful behaviors, then, conversely, there may be less dreadful behaviors that can be substitutes for suicide. And that topic—the topic of partial suicides, truncated lives, deaths of parts of the self—occupies the remainder of the volume.

Currently, the U.S. Army uses the recruitment slogan "Be all that you can be." The Army is talking about fulfillment, of using all of one's capacities. The opposite of being all you can be is living at much less than you could. This is the area of subsuicidal neurotic lives that Menninger loves to write about. And so do I. My concept of "subintentioned death" is a first cousin to Menninger's concepts of chronic, focal, or organic suicide. A *subintentioned death* is one in which the decedent has played a partial, latent, covert, unconscious role in bringing his or her death date forward, earlier than it needed to be. Menninger focuses more on lifestyle, on truncated, demeaned, pinched, and troublesome lives. Here is his outline: (a) *chronic suicides*, by which he means asceticism and martyrdom, neurotic invalidism, alcohol addiction, antisocial behavior, and functional psychosis; (b) *focal suicides*, under which he includes self-mutilations, malingering, polysurgery, purposive accidents, and impotence and frigidity; and (c) *organic suicides*, which he relates primarily to psychological factors in organic disease. It is a broad field that Franz Alexander—who was Menninger's psychoanalyst—would later call "psychosomatic medicine." What Menninger did in *Man Against Himself* was to psychologize the pathology of everyday life, all the way from a youngster's being "sick" to avoid going to school on examination day to an adult's going crazy to avoid "having" to commit suicide. Almost everyone in America became an amateur Freudian—most of them without being aware of it. Even hard-nosed scientists talked of (sibling) rivalry, (penis) envy, (castration) anxiety, and (Oedipus) complexes. Even in Peoria.

MAN
against HIMSELF

BY KARL A. MENNINGER

Harcourt, Brace and Company · New York
[1938]

CONTENTS

96

MAN AGAINST HIMSELF
PURPOSIVE ACCIDENTS

Further evidence as to the motives and devices of focal self-destruction accrues from the study of certain "accidents" which upon analysis prove to have been unconsciously purposive. The paradox of a *purposive accident* is more difficult for the scientific-minded person to accept than for the layman who in everyday speech frequently refers sardonically to an act as done "accidentally on purpose."

Indeed, it is probably upon the basis of an intuitive recognition of this paradox that superstitious fears have arisen with respect to certain "accidents," e.g., spilling salt, breaking mirrors, losing wedding rings, etc. These have become conventionalized and hence no longer capable of specific interpretation although they are sometimes taken seriously. The philosopher Zeno is said to have fallen down and broken his thumb at the age of ninety-eight, and to have been so impressed by the significance of this "accident" that he committed suicide (from which we might guess the unconscious meaning of the accidental fall and injury).

We must exclude from this category any conscious deception, i.e.,

---

From *Man Against Himself* (pp. 318–336), by K. A. Menninger, 1938, New York: Harcourt, Brace. © 1938. Reprinted with permission of Harcourt, Inc.

I picked this particular selection from Menninger's book because it illustrated, by its very topic, Menninger's omnipresent focus on the unconscious elements in everyday human life—even in so-called accidents. No area of living was exempt from his proactive search.

pretended accidents. But quite aside from this there exists the phenomenon of *apparent* (i.e., consicously) absent intention in acts which gratify deeper hidden purposes. I recall that I was once seated at a formal dinner by a woman for whom I had some dislike, which, however, I resolved to blanket completely so as not to spoil the conviviality of the party. I believe I succeeded quite well until an unfortunate piece of clever clumsiness on my part resulted in upsetting a glass of water over her gown into her lap. My dismay was the greater because I knew that she knew that "accidents [to quote from a recent insurance advertisement] don't happen; they are caused."

In many of these accidents the damage is inflicted not upon someone else but upon one's own self. The body then suffers damage as a result of circumstances which appear to be entirely fortuitous but which in certain illuminating instances can be shown to fulfill so specifically the unconscious tendencies of the victim that we are compelled to believe either that they represent the capitalization of some opportunity for self-destruction by the death instinct or else were in some obscure way brought about for this very purpose.

Such cases have been reported frequently. In one of his earliest case histories, Freud[1] cites an example of this. Herr K., a former lover of the patient, Dora, and latterly the object of her accusations and hostilities, came one day face to face with her on a street where there was much traffic. Confronted with her who had caused him so much pain, mortification, and disappointment, "as though in bewilderment and in his abstraction, he ... allowed himself to be knocked down by a car." Freud comments in this paper of thirty years ago that this is "an interesting contribution to the problem of indirect attempt at suicide."[2]

---

[1] Freud, Sigmund: *Collected Papers*, Vol. III, p. 145, London, Hogarth Press, 1925.

[2] *Collected Papers*, Vol. III, p. 145. Additional illustrations Freud gives in his *Psychopathology of Everyday Life* (London, Ernest Benn, Limited, 1914, pp. 198–209 and p. 216). The following is a striking example. A young married woman gave an exhibition of dancing one evening for an intimate circle of relatives. Her jealous husband was greatly annoyed, and reproached her by saying that she had behaved like a prostitute. After the incident she spent a restless night and the next morning decided to go driving. She chose the horses herself, refusing one team and demanding another. She refused vehemently to allow her sister's baby with its nurse to accompany her. During the drive she was very nervous and warned the coachman that the horses were getting skittish and finally when the animals "really produced a momentary difficulty she jumped from the carriage in fright and broke her leg, while those remaining in the carriage were uninjured." As Freud points out, the accident prevented her from dancing for a long time.

Abraham, also, in his *Selected Papers on Psychoanalysis* (London, Hogarth Press, 1927, pp. 58–62) cites numerous examples. One of these describes a girl who from childhood had an exceedingly strong affection for her brother. She grew to womanhood measuring every man by the standard of her brother, and had an unhappy love affair which left her depressed. Shortly after this she twice got into serious danger through her own carelessness on a climbing party, much to the wonderment of her friends who knew her to be a good climber, not likely to fall twice in safe and easy places. It appeared later that at this time she was in a hospital where she was accustomed to go for walks about the grounds; there was a ditch being dug in the garden which she used to cross by a plank bridge, although she could quite easily have jumped

The significant and differential thing about purposive accidents is that the ego refuses to accept the responsibility for the self-destruction.[3] In some instances, it can be seen how determined the ego is to make this evasion. This is sometimes ascribed by insurance companies and their attorneys to the wish to obtain double indemnity for the beneficiaries, but there must be more than this philanthropic motive back of it, even when it is conscious, and here I repeat that it is only *unconscious* purpose that I now have in mind.

If one thinks of his occasional hazardous blunders in street navigation, he is apt to ascribe them (if not to carelessness) to impulsiveness, absorption in other lines of thought, distraction, etc. But, after all, if one permits himself to so far relinquish interest in his own personal safety in favor of contemplating the stock market or the purchase of a new dress, one is certainly betraying self-destructive indifference to realtiy. And, as for impulsiveness, a volume could be written about the disasterous consequences of this symptom. It has ruined many a business, many a marriage, and many a life. The tragedy of Romeo and Juliet is, of course, a dramatic exposition of the way impulsiveness combines with hate to produce self-destruction. Romeo's impulsiveness lost him his sweetheart just before he met Juliet in the same mood. His subsequent impulsiveness first resulted in the death of his best friend (he started to intervene in the duel and did so in such a way as to allow his friend to be stabbed) and then, in the avenging of this death, his own exile. Finally, had he not been so impulsive in jumping to conclusions after he observed Juliet in the tomb and so precipitous in resolving upon suicide, neither his suicide nor Juliet's would have been necessary.

Someone might ask if such impulsiveness, granted that it be a symptom of imperfect psychological organization, is for that reason alone necessarily self-destructive in its purpose. We can only answer this by saying that experience shows that it is frequently self-destructive in its consequences; as to its origins, we have no right to speak with too much generality or definiteness. However, in numerous individual subjects the consequences of their impulsiveness has brought them into such serious straits

---

over it. At that time her beloved brother was to be married and this was much on her mind. On the day before his wedding, as she was out walking she sprang over the ditch instead of crossing by the bridge as usual, and did it so clumsily that she sprained her ankle. "Later on these self-injuries occurred so frequently that even the attendant began to suspect that there was something intentional in them. In these minor accidents her unconscious was obviously expressing the intention to commit suicide."

[3] The way in which the individual may be obliged to carry out the dictates of his super-ego through the utilization of "accident" is graphically illustrated in the following news item:

THREE WISHES

"In Detroit, Mich., Mrs. John Kulcznski said to John Kulcznski: 'I wish you'd go out and have an accident.' He was run over, lost part of a foot. Then Mrs. John Kulcznski said to John Kulcznski: 'I wish you'd lost the other foot.' He did. To stop Mrs. Kulcznski from wishing a third wish, John Kulcznski is seeking a divorce."—*Time*, March 26, 1934.

that they sought psychiatric treatment. We do know that the impulsiveness arises from an ill-controlled, partially disguised aggressiveness. This is almost transparently so in certain individuals who rush at their tasks or opportunities as if to sweep everything before them and, as they themselves sometimes put it, "to tear into it," only in the end to abandon the task prematurely or to make a botch of it in some way. They often appear to have the best of intentions but friends come to regard these as inconsequential bluffings. In love relationships viewed both from the psychological and the physical standpoint such prematurity is often extremely disappointing to both parties and its unconscious aggressive intent often suspected.

To turn from these clinical observations and theories to the matter of traffic accidents which have justifiably concerned all of those interested in public welfare in recent years, we now have statistical verification for the theory that certain individuals are more likely to have accidents than the average person. In a study of the street car motormen made in Cleveland, Ohio, by the Policy Holders Service Bureau of the Metropolitan Life Insurance Company, it was found that thirty per cent of the motormen on a certain division of the railway had forty-four per cent of all of the accidents. The National Safety Council has discovered this same propensity for accidents among automobile drivers. The people with four accidents were about fourteen times as numerous as they should have been on the basis of the theory that bad luck might be only pure chance, while people with seven accidents each during the time of the study were nine thousand times commoner than the laws of chance would require. Furthermore, those persons who had numerous accidents showed a pronounced tendency to repeat the same type of accident. "Chance plays but a small part in accidents" concludes this study by J. S. Baker,[4] engineer of the public safety division of the National Safety Council.

Automobile accidents often occur under circumstances which are suspiciously indicative of at least unconscious intent.[5] We sometimes say of a man who drives his car recklessly that "he must want to kill himself." Sometimes in the course of psychoanalytic treatment the evidence for a particular instance of this becomes convincingly great.

Patients frequently confess to conscious fantasies of "accidentally" driving their cars off cliffs or into trees in such a way as to make their death appear to have been accidental. Such as episode occurs, for example, in Michael Arlen's play, *The Green Hat*. One can only conjecture how

---

[4] Baker, J. S.: "Do Traffic Accidents Happen by Chance?" *National Safety News*, September, 1929.

[5] In the following double tragedy, for example, one can well imagine how the grief and a vicarious sense of guilt for the act of their son was related to the self-destructive accident of the parents, almost at the same spot. "A life for a life."

"At S——, N. Y., near where their son, B——'s car killed two in an automobile accident, Mr. and Mrs. X. Y. Z. were killed in their own car." (*Time*, November 10, 1930).

frequently fatal accidents are brought about through some more or less conscious suicidal intention.

That they are sometimes determined by unconscious suicidal impulses is suggested, for example, in a press clipping.[6] ... The National Safety Council computes the economic cost of accidental deaths, injuries, and motor vehicle damage to be approximately three and a half billion dollars a year. It would surprise many people to know that more men die daily in accidents than from any single disease except heart disease, and that accidents rank third among the causes of deaths to all persons in the United States. From the ages of three to twenty accidents kill more persons than any disease, and from the time he is three years old until he is forty a man is more likely to die of an accident than in any other way.

Every five minutes someone is killed in the United States in an accident and while one is being killed in an accident a hundred others are being injured. It is somewhat startling to think that while you have been reading these pages several people have been killed and several hundred others injured in our country alone.

Such statistics can only call our attention to the seriousness of the problem. Numerous plans are underway for reducing accident hazards in industry, traffic, agricultural life, and in the home. But all of these plans and the work of most of the agencies interested in the problem, it seems to me, fail to take into sufficient consideration the self-destructive element lurking unseen behind many "accidents."

In conclusion, it may be said that while some of the most dramatic illustrations of purposive accidents and of habitual victimization by "fate" are to be found in news journals, accurate and definite understanding of them awaits more detailed data. From pyschiatrically studied cases of this type, however, it is possible to make certain of the existence of the same motives familiar to us in other forms of self-destruction whether extreme (suicide) or partial (self-mutilations, compulsive submission to surgery, malingering). These motives include the elements of aggression, punition, and propitiation, with death as the occasional but exceptional outcome. The latter observation leads us to suspect that the principle of sacrifice is operative here so that in a sense the individual submits himself to the possibility or certainty of accidents in which he has at least a chance of escape rather than face a destruction which he fears even though it may threaten only in his conscience and imagination. In this way a partial neutralization of the destructive impulses is achieved. Meanwhile, practical interest in the very important problem of accidental death and injury is increasing, but thus far without benefit of research into this fundamental aspect of the matter.

---

[6]*Boston Globe*, September 5, 1932.

CHAPTER

8

BAECHLER
SUICIDES

Originally published in Paris, 1978

In my own efforts over the past 50 years to forge a clearer understanding of suicidal phenomena, it seemed to me that my mentor, Harvard Professor Henry A. Murray, in a few passing comments (embedded in other contexts), explained it best: "Suicide is *functional* because it abolishes painful tension . . . [it is a form] of relief from intolerable suffering"[1] and "Given intense and irremediable sufferings, there is nothing irrational about the act of suicide. It is irrational only to those who stand outside of it."[2]

But now along comes Baechler—who is not a psychiatrist, psychologist, or sociologist but a student of revolutions (!), a Maitre de Recherche at the Centre National de la Recherche Scientifique in Paris—studying suicide as though it were an individual revolution of some sort and producing one of the most insightful and analytic volumes on suicide that exists.

Adapted from a review, by E. S. Shneidman, 1980, *Contemporary Psychology, 25*, 108–109. Copyright 1980 by the American Psychological Association. Reprinted with permission.
[1]Murray, H. A. (1981). Outline of a conception of personality. In E. Shneidman (Ed.) *Endeavors in psychology: Selections from the personology of Henry A. Murray* (p. 216). New York: Harper & Row.
[2]Murray, H. A. (1981). Bartelby and I. In E. Shneidman (Ed.), *Endeavors in psychology: Selections from the personology of Henry A. Murray* (p. 491). New York: Harper & Row.

After mentioning and practically dismissing the three traditional approaches to the study of suicide—moral and philosophic analysis, the analysis of cases, and the use of statistics—he states that

> the problem of suicide must be taken up again on an entirely new basis. . . . I shall base my argument on the following definition: *Suicide denotes all behavior that seeks and finds the solution to an existential problem by making an attempt on the life of the subject.* (italics in original)

Essentially, suicide is a response to a problem; the center of suicidological investigation should therefore be the following question: "What kind of people seek what kind of solutions to what kinds of problems by means of suicide?" The formulation is breathtakingly simple and straightforward. It does not even implicitly assume a psychodynamic, social force, or epidemiologic point of view. It says about suicidal phenomena: Come, let us observe together, unbiased, from the *victim's* point of view.

After Baechler divides all previous approaches to the study of suicide into three types, as indicated above, he then implies that his book will be of some totally different genre, some new type. In fact, the book is essentially a case-by-case (127 of them) presentation. He views suicide as an intensely personal episode of behavior of *individuals* (as opposed to *types, groups,* or *high-risk clusters*) who "fail in their struggle for life." What is new in this book are his comments about suicide, his fresh ideas, and his iconoclastic approach to the topic—albeit from a traditional case study point of view.

Had Baechler stopped after his section on a strategic theory of suicide, he would have written only a first-class historical review without offering anything better than what now totally dominates suicidological thinking. But he has done much more. He has, with originality and flair, presented and explicated a new taxonomy of suicidal behaviors, built around his central idea of suicide as a "solution" to an inner or outer situation that is seen by the person as a problem.

In brief, Baechler proposes four kinds of suicidal acts or, to put it in his terms, suicidal acts among which four "typical meanings" (to the chief protagonist) can be distinguished: (a) *escapist* suicides, either of flight or of grief and punishment; (b) *aggressive* suicides, either of crime and vengeance or of blackmail and appeal; (c) *oblative* suicides of sacrifice and transfiguration; and (d) *ludic* suicides, involving the ordeal or the game.

An *escapist suicide* is one of flight or escape of a situation sensed by the person to be intolerable. This is because of a combination of felt emotions—shame, guilt, fear, worthlessness—or attendant to the loss of a central element of the individual's personality or way of life.

There are two subtypes: flight and grief. To my mind, most suicides are of the escapist type. The key word is *intolerable*.

Aggressive suicides are of four subtypes: crime (involving another's death), vengeance (to create remorse or approbrium), blackmail, and appeal (informing one's friends and family that the subject is in danger). But questions arise: Is this a cry for help? How does the last-named type differ from the need to escape from intolerable inner pain?

Oblative suicides of sacrifice or transfiguration are—says Baechler—"practically unknown in daily life." They relate to higher values or infinitely desired states. He is somewhat vague on this category, but the topics of seppuku and immolations of Buddhist monks must somehow be covered by this category.

The fourth major category is *ludic suicides*, in which he discusses the ordeal—to prove oneself—and the game. The relationship of "play" (carnivals, orgies, holidays, "unpluggings") to death and self-destruction is a fascinating and important topic. Baechler gives it serious consideration.

In his discussion of ludic (think of the word *ludicrous*) suicides —the ordeal and the game (Russian roulette being perhaps the best example)—he is especially original and intellectually entertaining. Of course, he refers to the work of Roger Caillois *Man, Play, and Games*,[3] but I cannot understand how he could fail to mention the classic *Homo Ludens: A Study of the Play Element in Culture* by Johan Huizinga.[4] Yet this is but a small lapse in this brilliant book.

I do not believe that the key question is whether or not Baechler has captured the absolutely optimal categories in his proposed phenomenological–existential taxonomy. I am sure that others will now rearrange, extend, rename, and improve them. More important, I believe, is whether or not he has opened our eyes to a new approach (with seeming important clinical and research implications), perhaps broader than any previous moralistic, psychodynamic, sociological, or epidemiological approaches or combinations of them. I believe that he has created a new genre of suicidology and that is his great achievement.

A suicidal event is certainly a genuine act, a solution to a genuine problem—but Baechler makes us realize that it may not always be a *cry* and that furthermore, whatever it is, it may be aimed toward various ends other than *help*: escape, revenge, sacrifice, testing the fates, and so on. Even so, Baechler's catholic and apsychological orientation is such that it permits him, unfortunately, to ignore the key

---

[3] Caillois, R. (1961). *Man, play, and games*. New York: Free Press.
[4] Huizinga, J. (1944). *Homo ludens: A study of the play element in culture*. Boston: Beacon Press.

concept of *ambivalence*, an omission that, to my mind, is a conspicuous and serious lacuna in his work and one of undeniable major consequence.

Baechler's great service, I believe, is not in his typology—which novices will quickly memorize (as they have memorized Kübler-Ross's purported five stages of the dying process)—but in the fact that he opens our eyes to the possibilities of other new and fresh conceptualizations of suicidal phenomena that stem from asking daring and fundamental questions. I take him seriously—and agree—when he generously says at the end of Part 2

> I am uncertain about the validity of my own types. I have distinguished 11 of them, which I have grouped together into four categories. It is perfectly possible that I have found too many or too few, that I have invented them where none exist, or that they are too coarse. I have yet to find the experiment that will allow me to verify my hypothesis. (p. 204)

And again—in his concluding paragraph of the book—he writes, "The problem itself was extremely difficult. It may well be that I have answered it badly. . . . I hope not to be the only beneficiary of the ordeal I have imposed on myself" (p. 457).

I can assure him that he is not. I was a beneficiary of his intellectual largess, and I recommend this book to my colleagues in suicidology and those who are interested in the creative study of humanity. This is a landmark book, clearly one of the dozen most important books written on suicide in the past 100 years.

SUICIDES

JEAN BAECHLER

With a Foreword by RAYMOND ARON

Translated from the French by BARRY COOPER

Basic Books, Inc., Publishers / NEW YORK
[1979]

CONTENTS

SUICIDES
ESCAPIST SUICIDES: FLIGHT

FLIGHT

To commit a suicide of flight is to escape by taking one's own life from a situation sensed by the subject to be intolerable.

EXAMPLES

Case 1

Rene G., 59, blinded in the left eye by a war wound, and partially deaf; five years earlier an attack of hemiplegia left his right side paralyzed. Slowly his condition worsened: he could no longer do any work and spent all his time lying down or seated in a chair. He needed assistance to attend to the smallest daily necessities. His character grew bitter; he became sad

From *Suicides* (pp. 66–75), by J. Baechler (B. Cooper, Trans.), 1979, New York: Basic Books. Copyright 1979. Reprinted with permission of Persius Books. (Originally published as *Les Suicides*, 1975. Paris: Calman-Levy.)

I picked this particular selection from Baechler's book because it is about escapist suicides, the focus of Baechler's own lively interest, and because it illustrates how he intermixes case vignettes with his own brand of sociopsychological analysis.

and irritable. He sensed himself to be—as in fact he was—a heavy and painful burden for his family. Under these conditions, and considering everything quite carefully, he decided to kill himself. He took advantage of the absence of his wife to take a razor in his left hand and try to slit his throat and right wrist. His wife found him on the floor, nearly unconscious. In hospital he declared his wish to die as an explanation for his action.

Case 2

Mr. M., 34. Treated since he was 20 years old for schizophrenia. Under treatment (insulin shock, neural-electric shock) he was perfectly stabilized and successfully resumed his job as inspector-general of a shipping company. During periods of stability he did not hide the fact that he was considered abnormal. Above all he suffered from not being able to marry. For his whole life the only thing that restrained him from suicide was fear of grieving an 88-year-old aunt and a 92-year-old grandmother. Even so, he made three attempts at killing himself in a period of ten years. He decided to commit suicide as soon as his aunt and grandmother died. He was unable to establish relations with others. "I cannot establish normal contact with them; people are nice to me out of pity. . . . I am alone and unmarried, and I cannot marry myself."

Case 3

Mr. Z., 52, a Spaniard. During a voluntary visit to hospital he got hold of a razor and deeply slashed his throat, which bled extensively and left a serious wound. Several days later he was ready to explain his gesture: "It was a fit of madness. . . . At times . . . I can't keep my head . . . I hear men's and women's voices telling me: you are going to be burned alive. . . . you rotten bastard . . . you will be shot with a gun, your house will be burned . . . all at once it got to me . . . I did it so I wouldn't hear them any more . . . to escape them!"

A Spanish refugee, he lived with his parents, now deceased, and then with his brother; he was unmarried; intellectual level rather low but quite active socially; mason. No psychopathic tendencies observed until he was five years old. Suddenly, he began to hear threatening voices that constantly repeated the same themes. That provoked suicidal tendencies in him. Then, for three years, "the voices no longer bothered me." A year later, they were back. This was the fit of madness "like an electric current." He tried to slit his throat with a knife. Hospitalized voluntarily for two months; the troubles continued. He left, and immediately underwent another hospitalization during which the above incident took place.

The seriousness of the act appeared to escape him: "I did not know what I was doing, I lost my head. It was because of the voices!"

Question: "You could have killed yourself!"
Answer: "You think so?"

Case 4

[Sabinin, specialist in plant physiology and organic chemistry, was dismissed from all executive positions in Soviet biology after Lysenko's victory in 1948.]

Sabinin was dismissed by Prezent immediately after the latter was named dean of biology at both the Moscow and Leningrad universities, and for a long time could not find work. After two years of wandering and of material and spiritual trials, with only occasional earnings, he was able, with the aid of friends, to obtain employment in the AS Soils Institute. But Oparin, then heading the AS Biological Section, and who fawned on Lysenko in every way, flatly refused to approve Sabinin's appointment, and he once more became an outcast. He had to leave Moscow and abandon his work on plant nutrition to study algae. But scientific journals would not publish his work. His brilliant, important book on plant physiology, on which he had worked for many years, was withdrawn from publication in 1948, just before it was due to see the light of day. Unable to bear such persecution, Sabinin shot himself in 1951. His suicide was a complete surprise to all his friends, who knew him as an optimist and man of self-restraint. I talked with him twice during that period, and he amazed me with his boldness and steadfastness. His position at the time was that of an unarmed man facing pirates of science armed to the teeth.

Case 5

But in his madness M. hoped to cheat his executioners, to run for it, to break away or be killed in the attempt—anything rather than die at their hands. It is strange that all of us, whether mad or not, never give up this one hope: suicide is the last resort, which we keep in reserve, believing that it is never too late to use it. Yet so many people who were determined never to fall alive into the hands of the secret police were taken by surprise at the last moment.

The thought of this last resort had consoled and soothed me all my life, and often, at times when things were quite unbearable. I had proposed to M. that we commit suicide together. M. had always sharply rejected the idea. . . .

The thought of suicide first came to him during his illness on the way to Cherdyn as a means of escaping death by shooting that he believed was inevitable. It was then that I said to him: "Very well, if they shoot us, we shan't have to commit suicide." At this, already ill and obsessed as he was, he suddenly burst out laughing: "There you go again." From then on our life was such that the suicide theme recurred frequently, but M. always said: "What . . . not now . . . we'll see. . . ." If he made up his mind to do it then, he would have been spared his second arrest and the endless journey in a cattle car to Vladivostok to horror and death in a camp, and I should not have had to live on after him.

Case 6

[*Perry Smith* is one of two hoodlums who massacred a family of four in Kansas in November 1959.]

And as was not uncommon when he was afflicted, he dwelt upon a possibility that had for him "tremendous fascination": suicide. As a child he had often thought of killing himself, but those were sentimental reveries born of a wish to punish his father and mother and other enemies. From young manhood onward, however, the prospect of ending his life had more and more lost its fantastic quality. That, he must remember, was Jimmy's "solution," and Fern's too. And lately it had come to seem not just an alternative but the specific death awaiting him.

Anyway, he couldn't see that he had "a lot to live for." Hot islands and buried gold, diving deep in fire-blue seas toward sunken treasure— such dreams were gone. Gone, too, was "Perry O'Parsons," the name invented for the singing sensation of stage and screen that he'd half-seriously hoped some day to be. Perry O'Parsons had died without having ever lived. What was there to look forward to? He and Dick [his accomplice] were "running a race without a finish line"—that was how it struck him.

One night he dreamed he'd unscrewed the bulb, broken it, and with the broken glass cut his wrists and ankles. "I felt all breath and light leaving me," he said, in a subsequent description of his sensations. "The walls of the cell fell away, the sky came down, I saw the big yellow bird" [the bird was part of a dream that had recurred since childhood; it saved him from a snake that was about to swallow him by whisking him up into the air].

Case 7

[The Gond are a tribe of India; polygamy brings with it numerous familial problems.] *Kawasi Dulga's* reaction was unusual. He appears to have been one of those husbands who should never have tried such an experiment; a man of weak character who could not keep his two wives in order. The women were always quarreling and made his home and life a misery. One day he went with the younger to the bazaar and, as they were coming home, they quarreled and Dulga slapped her. Presently he told her to go ahead as he wanted to relieve himself. She walked on a little way, but he did not appear and when she went back to look for him she found him hanging from a tree.

Case 8

[The Eskimo people, called the Chukchee, in northeastern Siberia, share with other Eskimos the custom today sometimes referred to as group sex or group marriage.] At present, group marriages are often concluded without any rite. One man simply says to another, "Let us be companions in wives." . . . Frequently, however, the wife stands for her right to select friends. I was told about one woman, who, being pressed by her husband to live with a friend whom she disliked, preferred to take her own life.

Case 9

[The Iroquois people in Quebec 1692] following a year of severe raids on the French settlements in the St. Lawrence valley, Governor Frontenac ordered burned two prisoners of the Five Nations . . . some charitable Person having thrown a Knife to them in Prison, he who had the least Courage of the two, thrust it into his Breast, and died of the Wound immediately . . . [the second] sung continually: "That he was a Warriour, brave and undaunted; that the most cruel kind of Death could not shock his Courage, that no Torments could extort from him any Cries, that his Companion was a Coward for having killed himself through feat of Torment."

Case 10

Mr. *Lee* was a clerk in a store in Yangchow. He was 29 years old and had four children, although his wages were only $10.00 per month, out of which he had to support his aged parents in addition to his wife and children. He found it necessary to borrow money and consequently fell heavily into debt. The high rates of interest charged made it impossible to repay the loans and he went even more deeply into debt. This fact caused him a great deal of worry. After several months, to cap his misfortunes, the store in which he was employed failed and he was thrown out of work. In his miserable dwelling the crying of his wife and children made him exceedingly sorrowful until finally in despair he jumped into the Grand Canal and was drowned.

Case 11

Bolubese, wife of one of the previous paramount chiefs of Kiriwina [in the Trobriand Islands], ran away from her husband to her own village, and threatened by her own kinsmen (maternal uncle and brothers) to be sent back by force, killed herself by *l'ou* [jumping out of a palm tree]. There came to my notice a number of similar cases, illustrating the tensions between husband and wife, between lovers, between kinsmen.

Case 12

An elderly [Joluo] woman [in Kenya], whose husband had died, depended on her children for sustenance. In old age she contracted a disease similar to leprosy. Her son, as is customary, on such occasions, destroyed her house in the compound and built one for her outside of the homestead. One morning they found that she had hanged herself because, they stated, of the pain and trouble she experienced through her illness and because she was so unhappy that she could not take her grandchildren to teach and love as was her role in life as a grandmother.

ANALYSIS

These cases were chosen because they seem to me to be suitable illustrations of what must be understood by *flight*. But they have not been chosen "too well" in the sense that one could easily enough produce other ones. The impression that eventually imposes itself is the one that I tried theoretically to establish above: suicide is a solution to a problem. Cases 1, 5, and 6 are particularly clear. Case 5 recalls a perennial truth: suicide is always available if we decide to throw in the towel. This proposition has a somewhat abstract and general significance. Cases 1 and 6 constitute, in contrast, a kind of personal balancing of accounts that ends up on the debit side. With each case, the solution is to obliterate the subject, the meaning of which is a flight: the subject refuses to continue to play the game. In order to be interpreted, a decision of this order does not require a complicated mechanism or an appeal to some deep and blind compulsion. The act itself cannot be called either normal or pathological: it is simply, from the subject's point of view, logical. Cases 2 and 3 illustrate this contention quite well: case 2 did not risk killing himself because suicide would be a compulsion or a corollary linked to schizophrenia as such but, quite simply, because schizophrenia progressively established itself, and the sick person had a more or less lengthy period when he could become aware of his condition and surmise that he could become only worse. It is possible that such a subject did not wish to court the risk and preferred to depart. Case 3 also is quite logical. When voices or monsters ceaselessly pursue you, it is logical that you would want to get away from them, and one way of doing so is suicide. It is not the act, which is only the solution, but the problem that is pathological. What is at issue is to know why and how an individual comes to suspect enemies everywhere and thus is able to invent phantoms who persecute him; in short, what is at issue is paranoia. But that the paranoiac flees into death has absolutely nothing mysterious about it. This is why the distinction between normal and pathological suicide makes no sense: *suicide is neither normal nor pathological: it is logical.* Clearly, this is not to say that the mental state of the suicidal person is one of indifference. From now on, and before considering any explanatory variables, one can suspect that the mentally ill are likely to be disproportionately represented among suicides of flight—not because they need to be mad to kill themselves but because they need to be mad to see the situation as so desperate that suicide remains the only solution. It is clear that, in reality, an individual rarely (not to say never) would have the lived experience of being pursued by implacable real enemies; it is more likely to find things of this sort in the imagination, that is, on the borders of paranoia.

It is appropriate at this point to recall what has already been said of the ambiguities of the suicidal act itself. It is false or at least one-sided to contend that the suicidal person is looking for death. To use Shneidman's terminology, one must distinguish cessation (total and definitive annihilation), termination (with hope of an afterlife), interruption (temporarily going out of circulation), and continuation (desire to be rid of something intolerable).

The third form, interruption, is quite appropriate here. In order to flee, one does not have to intend an absolute death; a relative and temporary death is sometimes enough. Here is a particularly clear case:

Case 13

Madame B. G., a 58-year-old widow; no prior psychiatric problems of note; in retirement for several years because of a disorder of the spinal column; this illness occasionally caused a great deal of pain in her back. For several months her family life was very tense because of a senile and authoritarian father. She was sent to a psychiatric clinic after having been hospitalized for an addiction to barbiturates. Upon admission, every trace of addiction had disappeared; the patient admitted that for several days she had been unable to sleep because of her back pains and especially because of the fights with her father, which had completely worn her out. Her only desire was to sleep, "finally to get some rest, no longer to see nor sense anything at all for awhile." This is why she first took five tablets of Noludar, then, when the first batch apparently were ineffective, another fifteen. Then she admitted she had developed a habit, especially when she was exhausted, of taking one or two tablets in order to sleep. She had already been hospitalized once for taking an overdose. The patient maintained that the thought of death did not even occur to her; but, on reflection she said that if per-chance so many tablets had made her die "after all, that would not have been terrible."

What clearly is involved here is neither an accident nor a death-wish but a flight to temporary and remissible nothingness. Sleep is, in fact, the best possible solution, and since the means for inducing sleep voluntarily exist, why not use barbiturates? Her final remark provides a key to the case, for it shows plainly that the goal looked for was flight from an intolerable situation (temporary, to be sure, but it did not much matter if it ended up permanent), not recuperation to deal once again with the tasks of daily life (people seeking to recuperate generally do not need barbiturates).

It is not necessary to construct a new type of suicide to interpret this case. Some writers propose the term suicide rest. This does not seem to be warranted. It is a good rule of thumb not to construct a new type except where the facts absolutely do not allow themselves to be subsumed under a type already available. Now the notion of a *rest* seems to be only a particular mode of flight determined by the different meanings that the sought-for death can take.

It is clear that the "decision" to take one's leave is made at a given moment. Nothing is served by declaring that it has been preceded by pressures, deceptions, tensions, and so on, that could induce an infantile regression. It remains true that at a given moment everything occurs as if a threshold had been passed, as if the subject judged that his cup was full. Now, no *objective* point exists that constitutes a threshold beyond which the game can no longer be won. It may be enough that a momentary fall leads one's entire capacity for living to melt away, that is, one's ability to confront difficulties; then the decision comes. It may be enough that an external and wholly fortuitous circumstance occurs at a precise moment so that the act is deferred, never to recur. The subject may somehow recover his spirits and find that he can respond to his problem in a positive way, or an unsuccessful decision may allow a sufficient lowering of tension to allow the problem to be reframed and reconsidered in a new and calmer light. In other words, in order to explain a single suicidal act, it is necessary to consider three variables: first, the real or imaginary problem as it is perceived by the subject; second, the personality of the subject in his capacities to respond adequately to his problem; and third, the decision itself. One can see the extreme complexity of the situation, and one suspects that it would be impossible to furnish an exhaustive account. In fact, on the first point, one can find a whole host of situations that could be presented either as a permanent datum for which there was no chance that there would be changes in a favorable direction (the cases of hemiplegia or paranoia) or as a temporary one for which there was every indication that it would unfold to the advantage of the subject. Between these two extremes, one could conceive and verify a whole series of intermediate situations. Thus, in the case of Sabinin, it is certain that the pressures brought against him by the Lysenko faction and by the Stalinist dictatorship were not a permanent and absolute datum. He killed himself in 1951. Had he waited an additional two years, the dictator would have died, and the general situation would have changed radically. Without rewriting the story of Sabinin's life, it is reasonable to think that the decision then would never have been taken. On the second point, it is clear that one must consider, as I have already said, the subject's capacity for resistance. There is no instrument in the world that can possibly measure what I would call the personal coefficient of resistance. But there is no doubt that it exists since, among individuals placed in similar situations, some kill themselves and some do not. All of Lysenko's victims did not kill themselves, nor do all paranoiacs, nor do all hemiplegics. The third point escapes all analysis. The decision to kill oneself is itself never observable; it is probable that even the subject cannot account for it. One must think of it as a hair-trigger, where consciousness plays a variable part.

This is why the suicide-type *flight* is one of the easiest to understand (in the sense of "putting oneself in the place of") and the most difficult to interpret. The factors that come into play are at this point so variable and unstable that each case represents an original constellation. This also is why the trigger mechanism is almost impossible to specify. One cannot know in advance if such a subject will or will not make a fatal decision. What is clearly signified is that the act is generally a surprise to one's friends and relations. How many times does one read: "I had no idea that . . ." or "it took me completely by surprise?" Contrary to what the almost inevitable but temporary feelings of guilt of friends and neighbors would lead us to believe, it does not follow from a lack of concern or coolness, but the genuine inability, even of the subject, to foresee the act. In the end, this is why an unsuccessful suicide may or may not try again. This is not a truism but a verification of our inability to know the future. Everything one can say simply summarizes generalities and clichés. One could say, for example, that, within the complex of the three variables that flow together towards the suicidal act (that is, the situation, personality, and decision), the more permanent and stable the situation is, the more probable a second attempt will be. Thus, for example, our paranoiac: if his condition were not to improve, he would in all probability try again, as would our hemi-plegic, unless he died of natural causes beforehand. A second attempt is likewise very probable in the case of initial schizophrenia from which the subject wished to escape by killing himself. As for the melancholic, there is practically no other way out. Consider Freud's definition: "The distin-guishing mental features of melancholia are a profoundly painful dejection, cessation of interest in the outside world, loss of the capacity to love, inhibition of all activity, and a lowering of the self-regarding feelings to a degree that finds utterance in self-reproaches and self-revilings, and cul-minates in a delusional expectation of punishment." Considering such a psychic state, it is not mysterious that the melancholic ends up always, so to speak, killing himself or at least attempting to do so. Nor is it mysterious that the act of suicide is very often preceded by a period of calm and serenity that friends and neighbors interpret wrongly as a return to health. Very simply, what is involved is the calm and lull that *follow the decision to kill oneself.* The subject has found his solution; it is certain that he had it at the back of his mind for some time and that the struggle needed to make the decision contributed to the aggravation of his condition. But once the decision was made, all his conflicts subsided and were replaced by a deceptive serenity. To be sure, if one can see why the melancholic commits suicide, one still does not know why there are melancholics. I am neither foolish nor naive enough to propose an interpretation when expert opinion is so divided. Indeed, it is not my problem. My problem is to try to explain why people commit suicide. In this sense, the suicide of the melancholic, as that of the paranoiac, is the easiest to interpret: he kills himself because it is the only solution remaining in him in order to flee a situation intolerable *to him*. In fact, one cannot very well see what other solution could be proposed except to hospitalize him or to put him in a position where the material possibility of killing himself was reduced.

To return to my present concern: one could maintain that the more unstable one's personality the more probable it is that a failure will be followed by one or more later attempts. Human nature being what it is, it is certain that sooner or later the subject's situation will again become a source of problems for him. Unfortunately, as we have said, we do not know how to measure the coefficient of resistance. Consequently, debate on this topic can only be retrospective and based on the suicidal act, by which one may infer an antecedent instability. This does not tell us much.

And finally, the last factor, the decision itself. It can be taken on the spur of the moment, the subject hitting on this solution without really reflecting on the seriousness of it. In the case of a failed attempt or an unexpected interruption (someone knocks on the door or the telephone rings at the precise moment when one is going to pull the trigger), it is probable that the postponed decision will never be taken up again. One could say that the coincidence of an otherwise barely troublesome, or at least transitory, situation with a personality whose resistance has been only temporarily lowered, and a sudden desire to kill oneself, is such an improbability that it is even more improbable that it will occur again in the same subject. From this conjunction of improbabilities arises the feeling of unease and even outrage that one experiences with people who were discovered and saved only by luck and of whom it is reasonably certain that they should never have given in at a moment of weakness and never would do so again. In the same way, there are accidents that are tied to a coincidence of circumstances that are both fortuitous and improbable so that, if they were once avoided, one can be certain that they will not return.

I cited a number of cases from non-Western societies. Those that I have been able to study have always been very briefly presented. That is, one cannot be certain of their interpretation, and it is possible that some of them should be included in an entirely different type-category. This does not much matter. The important point is that there is no reason to think that they are by nature different from Western suicides. Here, as there, we have a situation that gives rise to a problem; a personality confronting it decides to flee. The pattern is the same everywhere. What changes are the circumstances for which the pattern is only an abstraction. The problem that the poor Joluo grandmother had to deal with was a Joluo problem in the sense that it is determined by leprosy, the precautions that it requires of her kinsmen, and the role of the grandmother in that society. But in every society, no matter how different, one can find the same pattern. With us, a grandmother also can become ill, be hospitalized (that is, be separated from loved ones), and see herself deprived of her grandchildren's affections. On the other hand, it is hard to imagine a young woman driven to suicide because of the violence inflicted on her by her family to force her to live with a man she does not love. In this case, the structure of the family and the latitude left to women in their choice of husbands play an essential role.

These apparently insignificant remarks have their own importance. They enable us to avoid the possibility of speaking about suicide in terms of *causes* and *effects*. The suicide of the young Trobriand woman was not the effect of a cause that could be identified with the family structure of this society. Her suicide was the result of a decision taken by a determined personality in a situation created by a family structure. A different personality or a postponed decision would have forestalled suicide. It follows that is is absurd to consider society (or any aspect of society) as the cause of suicide. All that one can, and must, say is that society determines the situations that *can* lead to problems for *certain* people. Inversely, it is almost (I say almost because there are cases where the situation is purely imaginary) as absurd to refer all the factors back to the question of personality and neglect the real situations that people have to deal with, for that amounts to saying that, whatever the circumstances, the subject would have killed himself. In the majority of cases, that is clearly untrue. In good health, the hemiplegic or schizophrenic would not have killed himself; without family pressures, the unhappily married man would not have done away with himself. As for the decision itself, and the passage to the actual act, they depend on neither society nor personality: they are manifestations of human freedom in the sense that they are the effects of no cause and may as easily happen or not. Nothing in one's nature or one's environment forces a flight into death, but certain individuals, as a function of their nature and their environment, choose it.

A beautiful soul might be tempted to intervene here and suggest a remedy. It would be nice to construct a society where all occasions for suicide are removed (old age, sickness, misery, schizophrenia, melancholia, paranoia, family conflicts, etc.) so that unstable personalities (which, we would all agree, are a datum about which nothing may be done) would no longer have an opportunity to make such bad decisions. Of course, let us do what we can to decrease misery and sickness; let us care for the mentally ill; let us put an end to political power running wild and driving citizens to despair; let us find mutually agreeable solutions for our unfortunate differences, and so on. Broadly speaking, the contemporary West has, if not suppressed, at least considerably ameliorated, all kinds of situations that, at other times and in other places, put individuals into difficult situations. It would have to be shown that some sort of amelioration of suicides has also occurred. Nothing of the kind is evident. The only logical and solid conclusion is what I have already suggested: whatever the society, one cannot build one's life without effort or ability, and this inevitably leads to difficulties or failures. Like is not a dream but a test; flight by suicide accords us the opportunity of taking our leave at any moment.

9

AARON
THE INMAN DIARY: A PUBLIC AND PRIVATE CONFESSION

Originally published in Cambridge, Massachusetts, 1985

In my way of viewing things, the central reference, the basic text, for Arthur Crew Inman's diary is Harvard Professor Gordon Allport's 1942 monograph, *The Use of Personal Documents in Psychological Science*. In that slim publication, Allport—building on German philosopher Wilhelm Windelband's essential distinction between the *nomothetic* (tabular, statistical, demographic, epidemiological) approach to knowledge and *idiographic* (case history, clinical, autobiographical) approach to knowledge—asserts that the study of personal documents is a legitimate part of a science of psychology.

Personal documents include diaries, journals, logs, letters, confessions, and autobiographies. Inman's lengthy diary is a personal document *par excellence*. It is certainly grist for a psychologist's mill. It is an interesting fact that Allport's list of personal documents did not include suicide notes, perhaps the most personal, certainly the most poignant, of all self-penned documents. But that curious omission aside, there is still enormous methodological force in Allport's publication. Allport gives us permission to make a serious study of Inman's confessions and to call that study "legitimate" psychological science. Idiographic studies are one avenue to the direct, phenomenological study of the workings of the mind.

The Inman Diary provides us with an opportunity to examine aspects of the cultural and intellectual history of that time and place, specifically the United States in the 1930s, and more specifically, something of the fascist thread of the Nazi windstorm that was in the air. Inman's writings are of interest not only to today's psychologists but also to students of political science and historical practice.

Editor Daniel Aaron, professor of American studies at Harvard, tells us that he

> had to decide what to emphasize and de-emphasize, how to balance Inman's outrageous thoughts and deeds with his mitigating decencies and curious genius in this strikingly original work that has no counterpart in any literature he is aware of.

When he died in 1963 at age 69 by suicide, Inman left over 200 boxes of his typed diary to the Harvard library. Subsequently, Aaron spent 7 years editing this prodigious typescript (of 17 million words), first into 1,600 tightly printed pages—the two volumes of *The Inman Diary: A Public and Private Confession* and subsequently into a condensed paperback volume, *From a Darkened Room*. Aaron's work is a monumental effort.

The books are distinguished by Aaron's high scholarship: Inman the man is characterized by a number of repellent attributes. He is a hypochondriac, anti-Semite, Hitler-lover/FDR-hater, bromide addict, abusive husband, imperious employer, and generally wretched human being. What then are the possible virtues of the Inman diary. Simply put, they are the most openly candid and honest set of readily accessible 20th-century autobiographical materials we have of an individual who documented his suicidal thoughts over a span of years and then actually committed suicide. As such, the Inman volumes provide a fully explicated case history that is readily available to any serious student and can thus serve as a common source of data for multidisciplinary studies by any number of investigators.

Inman had excessively high aspirations for his diary. Aaron tells us in his introduction to the two-volume set that Inman (early in the 1920s when he was about age 25) decided that the only way for him to gain immortality was to write a diary unlike any ever written, "an absolutely honest record of himself and his age" (p. 1). Well into the diary (in 1927), Inman stated these goals explicitly:

> I have striven to portray myself. I have endeavored to give to posterity a true picture of American life and times. I have labored to turn out each entry with the utmost of workmanship at my command. I have been honest. I have held as my inspiration the in-

exorable judgment of an ideal posterity, the elite among them. It has been my wish to amuse, to instruct, to foster thought, to encourage action, to inspire men of genius to the full stature of their greatness. (p. 338)

What is impressive is the extent to which Inman remained faithful to his creed. If nothing else, at the end of his life, just before he committed suicide, he had earned the right to say "I have been honest." This is a diary in which, for the layperson's ears, we are often told much more than we really want to hear, but for our professional eyes we welcome the sight of a plethora of personal and historical details, even as we recognize the distorting lens of the projector.

The paperback edition of the diary is one-third the length of the two-volume set. What is omitted are Inman's ruminations about the South and about the Boston scene; his socioeconomic comments on American life, and his reports on international events, what he called "the vast and exciting panorama of history." Also deleted is an extraordinary 15-page medical report—not often seen in biographical accounts. In the abridged volume, Aaron provides us with a remarkable "cast of characters"—vignettes of the 38 people in this crowded drama, a cast large and florid enough to fill a thick Tolstoyan novel.

The number of extended diaries of autobiographical case histories in public print of individuals who committed suicide is not large. In the 20th century, the only serious rival to the Inman diary, in my opinion, is the published diary of prize-winning Italian writer Cesare Pavese. The Pavese diaries are available in English under two titles: *The Burning Brand* and *This Business of Living*. Compared with Inman, Pavese is a much more attractive person who claims our compassion. There are other published diaries of suicidal persons, but they are inferior in their psychological richness.

I shall try to avoid the vexing question of why people keep diaries, publish their autobiographies, leave suicide notes, or why, in general, people write about themselves at all. What I can say with some confidence is that there are no definitive answers to any of these questions.

I believe that any volume such as this that seriously intends to present a comprehensive view of 20th-century suicidology ought to include a representative of the personal, case history, idiographic approach to the topic of suicide—in addition to the biological, sociological, and psychodynamic views that dominate the field. There are materials in the Inman diary to capture the interest of a pharmacologist, geneticist, genealogist, biochemist, physician, sociologist, political scientist, social historian, Americanist, psychologist, psychoanalyst, linguist, logician, philosopher—to name a few kinds of specialists. I believe that every suicidologist should dip into *The Inman Diary*. I endorse the idea of suicidologists and behavioral scientists using the same case history materials, citing the exact paragraphs they are using to make their points.

For me, there are two difficulties in ploughing through Inman's diary: (a) his unattractive personal attributes—he stands for so many things that are anathema to me—and, (b) to be more professional, the vast amount of sheer psychological pain that he suffered which, even in this loathsome fellow, often claims a compassionate response.

It is not too difficult to taste the special flavor of this voluminous diary. One need only dip into it to sense immediately the alert, restless, self-centered, opinionated, intensely curious, candid, authoritarian, querulous mind at work.

For suicidologists, the most interesting items in Inman's diary are those that document his slide toward death. One major theme is the constant drum song of Inman's suicidal ideation—the siren call of the beguiling idea of death as an escape from pain. We can see over the years how the leitmotiv of general perturbation increases as Inman becomes older and genuinely more ill and, realistically, more helpless. It also seems evident that as Inman entered into what he thought of as old age, there was a confluence between the streams of death and suicide which, in the turbulence of their rushing together, was especially distressing to him and pushed his lethality over the fatal line.

One has to admit—that even in an odious way—Inman's diary is "the real thing." It is offensive, but it is not phony. In a paradoxical way, Inman's diary brings to my mind a sage observation by America's greatest psychologist, William James. In commenting about the secret workings of the mind and how best to mine them, James—in his *Varieties of Religious Experience*—said in 1903,

> Individuality is founded in feeling; and the recesses of feeling, the darker, blinder strata of character are the only places in the world in which we catch real fact in the making, and directly perceive how events happen and how the work is actually done.

The Inman Diary
A PUBLIC AND PRIVATE CONFESSION

Edited by Daniel Aaron

HARVARD UNIVERSITY PRESS
Cambridge, Massachusetts, and London, England
[1985]

CONTENTS

SELECTIONS FROM THE
INMAN DIARY

"Not growing in stature. I am painfully aware of how off-sized for my age I looked and how artificial and sissy I seemed. . . . It estamped me as outside my class, a scorned thing to myself and to others, a blasted tree. I felt then a failure, a person confined within myself." (Aug. 1912, age 17, p. 98)

"On a low type of man, such as the African Negro, the coccyx sticks out horizontally; on the average man it sticks straight down; and on a highly sensitized type like me it sticks in horizontally. . . . Their emotions are the emotions of a child." (Nov. 1919, age 24, p. 163)

"As I watched the receding campus through the rear window of a shaky old station cab, I felt very small, very tired, very lonely. If I could have foreseen ahead, I would have killed myself. Or would I have?" (1915, age 19, p. 129)

From *The Inman Diary*, by D. Aaron (Ed.), 1985, Cambridge, MA: Harvard University Press, two volumes, pages as noted in selection. Copyright 1985 by the President and Fellows of Harvard College. Reprinted with permission.

I picked these particular selections from Inman's diary because they seemed representative and because, taken together, they illustrated five of the constant themes in his diaries: suicide (which is on practically every page), Negroes/African Americans (960 entries in the two volumes), Roosevelt (140 entries), Jews (120 entries), and Hitler (80 laudatory entries). Of course, the entire selection illustrates the usefulness and importance of the intensive case study method.

"Exactly what is life worth to me? I hate life with a consuming and virulent hatred. I have always hated life, yet have never sought immediate and self-inflicted death for the very reason, I suspect, that to kill oneself were so vastly easy." (April 1925, age 30, p. 272)

"Jews are the hyenas of the world. They are made of mental and spiritual rubber. They bend but never break. . . . And their purpose? It is, I believe, to rule the world as Hebrew overlords. Are they not God's chosen people. . . . They are liars, thieves, cowards, rotten sentimentalists, voluptuaries. The race disgusts me individually and in toto." (May 1925, age 31, pp. 306–307)

"Someday when things become too difficult, I shall go under. I am resolved that whenever affairs force me against the wall I shall kill myself. But not yet." (Nov. 1926, age 31, p. 327)

"Another birthday. I am thirty-two. . . . It seems as though I have lived an eternity. Is there no end? Why do I not kill myself? Well, I do not. I live on, and year creeps laboriously after year." (May 1927, age 32, p. 336)

"You cannot realize the physical wreck I am, how lugubriously sensitive to every disturbance. I want to be dead. I am a craven to keep on living. . . . If I don't get away from noise soon I'll plain pop. Getting nearer and nearer to shooting myself. A finger on the trigger—then the end." (Aug. 1927, age 32, p. 341)

"I am practically crazy with my eyes. I cannot even see to write legibly any longer. I wake up every morning about four and lie awake trying to muster the guts to kill myself. I'll do it yet. I must." (July 1928, age 33, pp. 375–376)

"It has been two weeks since my heart commenced to go haywire, and I am as yet sitting up not two hours a day. Yesterday was the first day for three weeks that my bowels acted without an enema. My heart still pains grievously at times. Thoughts of doing away with myself were in my head. I wanted the pistol on the bureau. But how to get it? . . . Next morning I went after the pistol. My heart nearly collapsed in the effort, or so it felt. Anyway, I secured the weapon and put it in bed with me. I felt reassured and fell asleep." (Feb. 1932, age 37, p. 473)

"It is impossible to blame Hitler for his attitude toward the Jews. . . . I feel, with a qualm as to the wisdom of my feelings, that I wish to God every Jew and every Irishman and every negro and every Mediterranean and every Mexican could by some means be forced to leave this fair broad land of ours to us Nordics. . . . If Hitler can restore to the Germans a Germanic culture and a Germanic religion, the outright killing of six hundred thousand Jews in Germany would be worth the price." (April 1933, age 37, pp. 525–527)

"The face of Roosevelt is that of a bigoted and hypocritical minister of the gospel." (July 1934, age 39, p. 581)

"It is only by some mental or spiritual fluke that there is an entry today. I came closer to killing myself last night than ever before. I had the door locked and the cork on the chloroform bottle extracted, notes written avowing my responsibility, cotton for the chloroform. Then I backslid and here I am." (Nov. 1934, age 39, p. 602)

"I wish I were not so terrified of the inexorable vengeance of a cruel god meted out to those who take their own lives, of ill luck that would cause me to mangle myself if I attempted suicide." (June 1935, age 40, p. 633)

"I feel that it is no wonder that I fear death. For aught I know, eternal underworld dementia exists for the frenzied mind to wander in and never escape." (July 1936, age 41, p. 700)

"Nearly went wild yesterday. . . . My intelligence tells me that living here, with my sensitivity to noise, may become impossible. In simplest terms, the matter resolves to a choice between two decisions—either to kill myself and get out of all the woe that is ahead for me in life, or move. . . . When you look at it calmly, there's no reason why I can't aim calmly and pull the trigger firmly. I'm tired of evading life like a panicked rabbit." (Nov. 1941, age 48, p. 1042)

"I finally made up my mind last Saturday at about 8:45 in the evening, told Mrs. Cash I didn't want to read longer, kissed Evelyn good night. At 9:45 I commenced taking sleeping pills. I remember swallowing with water at five minute intervals seven 3-grain bembutol tablets and three 5-grain veronal tablets. Billy found me the next morning with an undissolved tablet in my mouth. I was out for forty hours. I regained consciousness (and a realization, vague but certain, that my efforts at self-destruction had failed) in a walled bed in what I was aware was a hospital." (Nov. 1941, age 46, pp. 1042–1044)

"I don't wonder I tried to bump myself off. This noise is almost unendurable to me. Less than three hours' sleep last night. . . . Almost anything at this juncture seems preferable to being kept awake from two to eight in the mornings, thus becoming conscious of a daytime noise I otherwise might forget. . . . It would be good to vanish from all consciousness forever. I wish I were dead." (Dec. 1941, age 46, p. 1047)

"The demonstration that is being put on about Roosevelt's death seems to me, rank sentimentalist though I am, sickeningly mawkish. . . . The volatile American people are wallowing in an emotional orgasm. . . . Well, Roosevelt is to be buried tomorrow at his estate at Hyde Park by the Hudson River, and I, for one, shall be glad to have him underground." (April 1945, age 50, p. 1269)

"To come to my worst woe, the one that's searing the pants off me, Huntington Avenue has to be repaved. All night long automobiles tore past what must have been sixty miles an hour. The vibration of the motors and the sound of the tires on the new pavement was so loud and so un-remitting that I couldn't get to sleep." (June 1948, age 53, p. 1409)

"I'm a fool and a fool and a fool, and I could shed tears that are long and pendant gray rain exuding from the heart of a sentimental idiot. I'm sad. I'm no good. I'm only as good (drunk me) as those who love me—love me for myself. Who is myself? A 'pile of shit' as Pearl says. More than that—I think. I am honesty and no false estimation. Into this world; into and out of it. A shithead with good intentions—me. I want to be good, to be helpful, to be a person devoted to helping others. Am I? Who knows? I am solitary, poopish, frightened Artie. That's me." (1956, age 61, p. 1563)

"These mornings are long in passing. It's as if they are the tide going out on a shallow beach. And the years creep like a tortoise. I suppose that, does one hoard and count the years, the mornings pass like driven spume. It is nineteen years since I tried to kill myself, and even then it was as if I had persisted a thousand years. Yet here I am, a thousand years added, still in function, however piddling." (Dec. 1960, age 65, p. 1584)

"I am a man. I am an animal. I am no more, no less, despite my mind, than animal. If I am no more than animal, then as animal dies and amounts only to manure for other forms of life, so do I. . . . What difference if I die a natural death or perish by my own desperate hand. . . . I'd rather die than be uprooted and set down somewhere else, my roots torn and broken and strained. Perhaps I may find what's ahead so unbearable as to make the final course a matter of hara-kiri courage." (March 1961, age 66, pp. 1587–1588)

"However silly I am, big tears roll down my far-too-seeing eyes. Here goes America, with its confidence and its pride; here goes America with its abdication to credit and purblind destruction of its shaped past. . . . This is where one of my generation should die, be dead. From here on the sanctity of the individual goes by the board. I would be better off not here." (Sept. 1962, age 67, p. 1592)

"Jumping out of my skin with nervousness from the nearer and nearer demolition, motors racing, walls falling (the ball is being used), the build-ing shaking and creaking. . . . With every building demolished, new electric lights and signs are let free to shine into my sitting room where it is so bright I have to shield my eyes with something to raise the window opened at night. As soon as the buildings opposite my bedroom are down, God knows what shafts of light will shine in on my walls past the curtain I tie out at night to get air. I feel a Medieval baron in his besieged keep, forces and weapons constricting ever tighter around his security. It may be I'll survive this, but then again I may not, now that D-day is here, to survive within the limits of my disposable defenses. My truest weapons are designed by ingenuity. They are indeed my final weapons. Until tested, who can know their temper?" (March 1963, age 67, p. 1596)

Note: Later that year (1963) Inman took 15 sleeping pills and was hospitalized. He found the hospital noises soothing "not like the angry noise of trucks going up hill near where I was."

Here are further snipets from his diary: November 1963—"I feel a harried ninety years old with gathering pressures closing in about. I have lived too long. I have written too much." December 3—"I feel like the tag end of a rough time." December 4—"This has truly been, is a session in hell. Eight migraines yesterday, and one more at six this morning, with violent headaches and nausea." On December 5 he scrawled a message: "This is being horrible beyond the credible. Twelve divisions of migraines. Idetic images until I am harried and frightened into desperation. Can't see more than is adequate to get around. Everything overgrown with hands and the imaginary element of substance visible."

The next day, December 6, 1963, at age 68, he shot himself.

In the published diary, Aaron has appended a medical report by David F. Musto, MD. After listing 23 medical illnesses that Inman complained of, Dr. Musto concluded,

> A review of Arthur Inman's medical history from the start of his in- validism leaves little doubt that his life—leaving out his singular per- sonality—was cruelly complicated by medical maltreatment and by excessive, chronic ingestion of bromides, alcohol, and other powerful chemicals. These attempts to cure had almost without exception a destructive effect on his emotional stability, judgment, and physical health. And yet, his illness had a positive aspect. . . . The secondary gain was so great and solved so many of his emotional problems that he had little incentive to change his style of life. He persisted in his goal to write a response to the times in which he lived, and he suc- ceeded. Under the envelope of illness, Arthur Inman had an indomi- table will; it is in this interplay between sickness and creativity that his fascination lies.

10

MALTSBERGER AND GOLDBLATT
ESSENTIAL PAPERS ON SUICIDE

Originally published in New York, 1996

In the past several years, the New York University Press has published a series of books on various aspects of psychiatry under the general heading of "Essential Papers." Their most recent—the 15th in this series—edited by John T. Maltsberger and Mark J. Goldblatt —is entitled *Essential Papers on Suicide*. An exact listing of the 40 items contained in that bushel basket of intellectual goodies is given in the table of contents. For Maltsberger and Goldblatt to put forward such a list of the 40 essential papers on this complicated, vexatious, and contentious topic is not only a feat of high scholarship, but also an act of considerable bravery. It takes courage for two suicidologists, no matter how impressive their own credentials, to tell their fellow suicidologists who is "in" and who is not; that *this* is *the* list; that, bibliographically speaking, here is what 20th-century suicidology *is*. They tell us in their introduction:

> Our purpose in this collection is to offer an array of papers that are psychologically close to the suicide experience, or else throw light on that experience, ... If these papers are essential, it is because they deepen our grasp of the texture and color of the inner lives and struggles of suicidal patients and the corollary challenges they pose for those who treat them.

In a general sense, Maltsberger and Goldblatt's book addresses the question, What clues to suicidal events—to their etiology and mollification—can we glean from the psychiatric and psychological literature published in the 20th century?

Here are some of my reactions to the contents of the book—eschewing the topics of obvious omissions and unnecessary inclusions—about groupings of papers, implications for therapy, views of the suicidal act, and what we are supposed to learn about suicidological theorizing.

After making obeisance to Freud's indispensable 1917 paper on "Mourning and Melancholy" in the preface—and saying that they did not reprint it because it is easily available elsewhere—Maltsberger and Goldblatt then reprint, with instructive comments, the 40 selections, chronologically, beginning with Ernest Jones's 1911 paper relating suicide to birth and death. Then follow important papers by Karl Menninger, Gregory Zilboorg, and two score of other worthies including Robert Litman, Aaron Beck, Marie Åsberg, Herbert Hendin, and Jan Fawcett.

At first reading I felt overwhelmed by the plethora of intellectual richness, but then I saw that the papers might sensibly be divided among five categories: (a) papers about affective states; (b) papers relating to psychiatric diagnostic categories, physiological changes, or demographic indicia; (c) papers discussing the therapist or the family; (d) papers about the biology or possible genetics of suicide; and (e) papers concerning psychodynamic formulations. A few words about each.

1. *Affective states.* These included papers touching on such topics as hopelessness, loneliness, anxiety, depression, despair, fear, anguish, aggression, and anhedonia—11 such pieces.

2. *Diagnostic categories, physiological measures, demographic indicia.* There are around 20 papers in this category. They include papers centered on suicide and schizophrenia, depression, alcoholism, melancholia, borderline disorder, panic state, affective disorder, abnormal spinal fluid values, masochism, abandonment, somatic illness, family history of suicide, preoccupation with death, special vulnerabilities, lack of exterior resources, death fantasies, and poor reality testing. Many of these papers seemed to hover around the spirits of the two Emiles: Emile Kraepelin (alive today in the *Diagnostic and Statistical Manual of Mental Disorders*) and Emile Durkheim's *Le Suicide*, which explored the power of the

nomothetic approach in suicide. It is not my opinion alone that these are 19th-century masterpieces, but it is my belief, perhaps idiosyncratic, that they are both outworn and are being systematically misapplied, almost a century later, in clinics, hospitals, and other health management organizations everywhere.

3. *The therapist, the family.* There are fewer than one handful of papers in this category; specifically, papers on the role of transference in psychotherapy, on countertransference hate, on the importance of consultation in treating suicidal patients, and on the role of death wishes within the family. The importance of significant others and of community resources is underrepresented in the technical literature on suicide.

4. *Biology of suicide.* In this category, two important papers are reproduced. They are Alec Roy's "Family History of Suicide" and "5-HIAA in the Cerebrospinal Fluid: A Biochemical Predictor?" by Marie Åsberg and her Swedish colleagues.

5. *Psychodynamic formulations.* By far the largest number of papers—about 35 of them (remembering that some papers fell into more than one category)—were discussions of some psychodynamic constellation that, it is asserted, underlies the commission of suicide. It is alleged in serious venues, mostly psychoanalytic journals, that suicide can be seen as related to homicide, as associated with birth and death, as reflected in the wish to kill and the wish to be killed, as murderous aggression toward the self, as revenge, as spite, as reflected in fantasies of escape, as a discharge of aggression, as a ritual phenomenon, as related to the wish to sleep, as fusion with the other, as reunion with the dead, as a wish to be reborn, as narcissistic exhaustion, as abandonment, as an unconscious wish to be eaten, as confusion of self and others, and as atonement. In addition, suicide is discussed in terms of ambivalence, rescue fantasies, its dyadic nature, its erotic elements, and death instinct.

All of these formulations, a priori, might be true—or none might be true. It is certainly food for thought, and they have sometimes been the main course in banquets of psychotherapy, but I am not yet satisfied that the enduring proteins, carbohydrates, and vitamins of suicide prevention are contained in that menu.

It may well be that those 40 authors were not only examining very different parts of the beast—the trunk, the tail, a leg—but that it was not an elephant in the first place. It may have been a unicorn, in which case they certainly missed looking at its distinguishing horn that, in its pointed convolutions, may contain the magical elixir of knowledge.

Here is my summary of those 40 items contained in *Essential Papers on Suicide*: In the 20th century, suicidologists (mostly psychoanalytically oriented psychiatrists) seem to have written about four psychological aspects of suicide:

1. *Fight.* These are papers on suicide as murder, aggression, rage, anger, spite, rejection, revenge, the wish to kill. This thread has been overemphasized, in my opinion. Suicide can be other than homicide; the principal emotional state can be other than murderous rage.

2. *Flight.* These are papers on suicide as escape, rescue, sleep, rebirth, reunion, the wish to die, and as an effort to escape unbearable consciousness. This category represents the majority of my own voices on the principal meaning of suicide.

3. *Fright.* These are papers on suicide as painful loneliness, isolation, abandonment, hopelessness, anxiety, confusion, panic, psychic pain. In general, important opportunities for remedial action lie in this category.

4. *Freight.* These are papers on a family history of suicide, hatred in the family, scapegoating, history of abuse, mental illness in the family, genetic vulnerability. These are the onerous psychological burdens that one carries on one's shoulders, none conducive to running life's race in the happiest style.

The Maltsberger and Goldblatt book is important. The book itself is essential, but like many essential items in life, it nonetheless leaves us hungering for other templates, radically different approaches to suicidal phenomena. Some years ago, responding to some needs I felt —order? understanding?—and in an effort to be a more effective therapist with suicidal persons I was then treating at the University of California, Los Angeles, Neuropsychiatric Institute (where I was a professor for some 20 years), I prepared, on one sheet, a list of Henry A. Murray's psychological needs—taken from Chapter 3, ''Aspects of Personality,'' of Murray's monumental *Explorations in Personality*. After a therapy session, I would rate the patient, distributing exactly 100 points among the 20 need categories.

I made these ratings after each session so that I could monitor the flow of the therapy. This simple form—admittedly a profanation of Murray's 100 pages of finely stenciled text—gave me a new format, a fresh conceptualization, another template for understanding my patient's dialogues with suicide—what Murray had called "the full Congress of the mind." I have always felt that the therapist's understanding of a concept is propaedeutic to any consistent psychotherapy. Psychotherapy is not just a hierarchical conversation; therapy goes much better if there is a clear conceptual template in the therapist's head. I thought then and believe today that I had found mine in *Explorations in Personality*.

In retrospect, in almost every case I have ever seen, it appears that suicide is pushed by pain; suicidal fantasies and acts are efforts to escape or put a stop to the pain that flows through the mind. It is a special kind of pain, psychological pain, the pain of the negative emotions—guilt, fear, shame, defeat, humiliation, disgrace, grief, dread, woe, loneliness, hopelessness, frustrated love, fractured needs, rage, hostility, and the perception that the pain is unbearable. For the suicidal person, that psychological pain, that pain in the mind, that *psychache*, has an intensity that pushes it into a special qualitative state; it is deemed unbearable, intolerable, unacceptable; it has crossed a certain critical line somewhere in the mind (see E. S. Shneidman, *The Suicidal Mind*. New York: Oxford University Press, 1996).

These are some of the reflections I could not have had if I had not been mesmerized and catalyzed by the cornucopia of thoughts contained in *Essential Papers on Suicide*. From my own experience with this endlessly stimulating volume, I cannot believe that any thoughtful reader can peruse these two-score papers (and read the editors' thoughtful comments) without significant inner growth.

Essential Papers on Suicide

edited by
John T. Maltsberger, M.D., and
Mark J. Goldblatt, M.D.

NEW YORK UNIVERSITY PRESS
New York and London
[1996]

CONTENTS

ESSENTIAL PAPERS ON SUICIDE

INTRODUCTION

Though suicide has not one cause, but many, they all flow together into one river whose overwhelming current, mental pain, carries everything before it. Those doomed to it choose death over intolerable suffering that to them seems interminable. Few have better described the anguish that leads to suicide than William Styron (1990), the title of whose autobiographical memoir of near-suicide, *Darkness Visible*, comes from Milton's vision of Hell. Do theological writers draw their vision of damnation from intuitions of depressive suffering? Poets and artists are prey to it (Jamison 1993), but so are multitudes of others. Hundreds of thousands of patients tremble in depressive anguish, and many are carried away into suicide. More than thirty thousand persons commit suicide every year in the United States alone.

Though suicide, after accidents and HIV infection, destroys more young people in the United States than anything else, it is neglected in

From *Essential Papers on Suicide* (pp. 1–8), by J. T. Maltsberger & M. J. Goldblatt (Eds.), 1996, New York: New York University Press. Copyright 1996 by New York University Press. Reprinted with permission.

I picked this particular selection from Maltsberger and Goldblatt's book because, like the selection from Stoff and Mann's edited volume, it is an introduction and overview that sets the tone for the entire volume (of 40 "essential papers" from the 20th century). It reminds me of this present volume.

145

medical education. Mainstream physicians and surgeons know little more about it than the general public (Murphy 1975). Many psychiatrists have not been well educated about suicide. In psychiatric residents' education considerable biological and psychopharmacological attention is paid to those disorders under whose rubrics suicide is most likely to occur (affective disorders, alcoholism, and schizophrenia), but the clinical phenomena immediately surrounding suicide are scanted. Trainees are taught to tick off items in the *DSM IV* checklist for the major depressive syndromes, but they are not taught how to assess depressive anguish. Indeed, anguish is not even listed among the criteria for diagnosing depression in the standard nomenclature (American Psychiatric Association 1994, 327). There we find "depressed mood" and "diminished interest or pleasure" mentioned, but nothing explicit to direct attention to the howling wind of depressive agony (see Shneidman, chapter 40 below). Unconscious forces in suicide are increasingly neglected in training programs, and so are family dynamics, dreaming, psychotherapeutic treatment, the quality of object relatedness, and careful diagnostic interviewing.

We hope this volume will help clinicians concentrate their attention on those suicide phenomena they may have overlooked, and that it will help readers to come empathically closer to those who are shaken by the terrible forces of suicidal illness.

The study of suicide has eighteenth-century roots, but only in the last thirty-five years has it grown robustly. Jean Esquirol (1772–1840), psychiatrist of the French Revolution, led the way in medicalizing insanity. While working to draw patients out of prison conditions into circumstances of humane care Esquirol devised a classification of mental disorders suggested by the work of Linnæus, the famous plant taxonomist of the Enlightenment. Suicide had a prominent place in Esquirol's studies, claiming a chapter in his *Treatise on Insanity* (1838).

If Esquirol medicalized suicide Émile Durkheim (1858–1917) sociologized it, explicating it in terms of society's tendency to integrate its members (or not), and to regulate the way they think, feel, and act. His celebrated *Le Suicide* (1897) is much cited. A short time later Sigmund Freud and his followers psychologized suicide. A few years after Durkheim's treatise appeared the Vienna Psychoanalytic Society took up the subject. Their 1910 discussions concerning student suicide were subsequently published (Freidman 1967). Freud's (1917) "Mourning and Melancholia" appeared seven years later and concentrated psychiatrists' and psychologists' minds on the unconscious turning of aggression against the self. So strong was the influence of this paper that it overshadowed psychodynamic studies in suicide for the next forty years.

Important as these developments were, the earlier contributions to our understanding of suicide were not frequent, and their appearances were spread over a span of many years. Suicide studies began to be published frequently only a little more than three decades ago, partly because funding for psychiatric research was more freely available at the time, and partly because of the imagination and leadership of Edwin Shneidman, Norman Farberow, Robert Litman, and others who established the Los Angeles Suicide Prevention Center.

The year 1958 was a critical moment in the development of suicide studies. That was when the Los Angeles Suicide Prevention Center (LASPC) opened its doors (Shneidman and Farberow 1965). The energetic core professional staff of the LASPC, a multidisciplinary collaboration, published a number of important papers and accumulated such momentum that more and more people from various portions of intellectual and public-spirited life grew enthusiastic about understanding and preventing suicide. Shneidman invented a new word to suit the times—*suicidology*; the study of suicide and related phenomena.

In 1968, after a Chicago meeting of a number of eminent scholars from different disciplines who were concerned with suicide prevention, Shneidman took the lead in founding the American Association of Suicidology. The Association established a journal devoted to suicide and related subjects (*Suicide and Life Threatening Behavior*), which has served to stimulate interest in and inseminate suicide studies ever since.

In the past thirty-five years what began as a trickle of suicide-related papers has swollen to a flood. The American Suicide Foundation, incorporated in 1987 under the leadership of Dr. Herbert Hendin, now funds suicide research across the United States, and promises much for the growth of suicidology and the future treatment of suicidal patients.

The publication of *Essential Papers on Suicide* comes at a time when the annual publication of suicide material is overwhelming, yet much that appears is clinically remote. It has become difficult to recognize and retrieve many contributions useful in the actual care of suicidal patients. Many good papers molder on the back shelves of libraries. Some of them, having appeared in out-of-the-way journals, are difficult to find. In offering this book we hope to draw attention to some of the best papers and to present them in one volume that will come readily to hand, relieving students of burdensome searching through bookstacks of old bound (and new unbound) volumes when they wish to study or revisit some promising source.

This anthology is not intended to offer a fair sampling of the current literature, a flow continuously supplemented by tributaries from sociology, philosophy, epidemiology, neurochemistry, and other disciplines. We do not underestimate the impressive waters of the suicidological river. For the most part, however, they swirl far from everyday clinical practice. This volume of "essential papers" is intended for clinicians who have no time to swim about looking for what might help them in their work. Specifically, these papers have been selected as aids in *understanding* suicidal patients.

Although there are no psychopharmacological studies here, we do not intend to minimize the value of psychopharmacological and biological contributions. We emphasize, indeed, that adequate treatment of suicidal patients usually involves a broad approach to their problems, one aspect of which is psychopharmacological.

The development of anti-depressant drugs represents the major therapeutic advance in helping suicidal patients in recent years. However, most psychopharmacological papers pertain to the treatment of depression and other psychiatric illnesses in general, and not to suicide specifically.

The controversy that arose concerning fluoxetine (Prozac) soon after it was introduced in the United States seems to have died down (Teicher, Glod, and Cole 1990). All medicines cause some side-effects. The overwhelming majority of psychiatrists believe that anti-depressants are extremely helpful in treating depression. Some depressed patients may worsen while taking anti-depressant drugs, either because they develop a certain restlessness known technically as *akathisia*, or because they experience an increase of energy that precedes improvement in their suicidal mood (Rothschild and Locke 1991). In the absence of improved mood, the increased energy may impel a suicide attempt (the depression is getting better, but the suicidal attitude has not improved as fast as the level of energy). No one anti-depressant drug has been proven superior to others in the treatment of suicidal patients. Readers who wish a fuller discussion of the psychopharmacological treatment of depression (most suicidal patients are indeed depressed) may find some of the following references of interest. Herman M. van Praag and his colleagues have edited an excellent volume on the psychobiology of violence and suicide that is of great interest (van Praag, Plutchik, and Apter 1990). The drug treatment of mood disorders has recently been reviewed by Pedro L. Delgado and Alan J. Gelenberg (1995). Mark J. Goldblatt and Alan F. Schatzberg (1990) have reviewed the psychopharmacological treatment of depression as it applies to suicidal patients. There are several outstanding textbooks of psychopharmacology now in print that cover this subject admirably (see, e.g., Schatzberg and Nemeroff 1995).

Our purpose in this collection is to offer an array of papers that are psychologically close to the suicide experience, or else throw light on that experience, whether the papers are biological, chemical, or sociological. Our bias is, in short, psychoanalytic. We believe that a good grasp of the psychology of suicide, and of the special emotional challenges that confront those who treat suicidal patients, is the *sine qua non* for effective clinical work, whatever psychotherapeutic or psychopharmacological tactics one may embrace. If these papers are essential, it is because they deepen our grasp of the texture and color of the inner lives and struggles of suicidal patients and the corollary challenges they pose for those who treat them.

. . .

With the expansion of suicide studies over this century we understand the inner lives of suicidal patients much better than before. The papers gathered here have been selected to reflect this knowledge, to put it into a more general psychiatric perspective, and to provide clinicians with the best possible foundation from which to proceed constructively. We commend them to you and trust you will find them helpful.

REFERENCES

American Psychiatric Association, 1994. Diagnostic and Statistical Manual of Mental Disorders. *4th Edition. Washington, D.C.: American Psychiatric Association.*

Delgado, P. L., and Gelenberg, A. J. 1995. Antidepressant and Antimanic Medications. In Gabbard, G. O., ed., Treatments of Psychiatric Disorders. *Washington, D.C.: American Psychiatric Press.*

Durkheim, E. 1897. Le Suicide. *Spaulding, J. A., and Simpson, G., trans.* Suicide: A Study in Sociology. *Glencoe, Ill.: Free Press, 1951.*

Esquirol, J. E. D. 1838. Des Malades Mentales. *Hunt, E. K., trans.* Mental Maladies, a Treatise on Insanity. *Philadelphia: Lea and Blanchard, 1845. (The English translation was reissued in a facsimile edition in 1965 by the Hafner Publishing Co., New York.)*

Freud, S. 1917. Mourning and Melancholia. *Standard Edition 14:239–260.*

Friedman, P., trans. 1967. Discussions of the Vienna Psychoanalytic Society— 1910. On Suicide, with Particular Reference to Suicide among Young Students. New York: International Universities Press.

Goldblatt, M. J., and Schatzberg, A. F. 1990. Somatic Treatment of the Adult Suicidal Patient: A Brief Survey. In Blumenthal, S. J., and Kupfer, D. J., eds., Suicide Over the Life Cycle: Risk Factors, Assessment, and Treatment of Suicidal Patients. *Washington, D.C.: American Psychiatric Press.*

Jamison, K. R. 1993. Touched with Fire: Manic-Depressive Illness and the Artistic Temperament. *New York: Free Press.*

Milton, John. 1667. Paradise Lost. In The Poetical Works of John Milton. *H. Darbishire, ed. London: Oxford University Press, 1958.*

Murphy, G. E. 1975. The Physician's Responsibility for Suicide. II. Errors of Omission. Annals of Internal Medicine 82:305–309.

Rothschild, A. J., and Locke, C. A. 1991. Re-exposure to Fluoxetine after Previous Suicide Attempts: The Role of Akisthesia. Journal of Clinical Psychiatry 52:491–493.

Schatzberg, A. F., and Nemeroff, C. B., eds. 1995. The American Psychiatric Press Textbook of Psychopharmacology. *Washington, D.C.: American Psychiatric Press.*

Shneidman, E. S., and Farberow, N. L. 1965. The LA SPC: A Demonstration of Public Health Feasibilities. American Journal of Public Health 55:21–26.

Styron, W. 1990. *Darkness Visible: A Memoir of Madness. New York: Random House.*

Teicher, M. H., Glod, C., and Cole, J. O. 1990. *Emergence of Intense Suicidal Preoccupation during Fluoxetine Treatment.* American Journal of Psychiatry *147:* 207–210.

Van Praag, H. M., Plutchik, R., and Apter, A., eds. 1990. Violence and Suicidality. *New York: Brunner/Mazel.*

V

INSIGHTS ON SURVIVORS
AND VOLUNTEERS

11

CAIN
SURVIVORS OF SUICIDE

Originally published in Springfield, Illinois, 1972

Some years ago, in the book *On the Nature of Suicide*,[1] I noted a number of conceptual developments, trends of practice, and emerging patterns of research within contemporary suicidology. Among these were (a) "the key role of 'the significant other' in the suicidal dyadi and the growing view of the suicidal crisis as a dyadic crisis" and (b) a new appreciation of the importance of what Harvard psychiatrist Erich Lindemann had earlier labeled "preventive intervention" and what I had called *postvention*—that is, work with the survivor–victims of a committed suicide to help them with their anguish, guilt, anger, shame, and perplexity. Albert C. Cain's book, focusing as it does on the survivors of suicide, invites our attention to the largest mental health casualty area related to suicide: the traumatically created widows and orphans—in short, the benighted victims of someone else's suicidal act.

In the passionate epilogue to *Man's Concern with Death*,[2] the eminent English historian Arnold Toynbee—then in his 80s—makes the point that death is essentially a dyadic event:

---

[1] Shneidman, E. (Ed.). *On the nature of suicide*. San Francisco: Jossey-Bass.
[2] Toynbee, A. (1968). *Man's concern with death*. New York: McGraw-Hill.

> There are always two parties to a death; the person who dies and the survivors who are bereaved. . . . The sting of death is less sharp for the person who dies than it is for the bereaved survivor. This, as I see it, is the capital fact about the relation between living and dying. There are two parties to the suffering that death inflicts; and in the apportionment of this suffering, the survivor takes the brunt.

In cases of absolutely sudden and unintentioned deaths, the total sum of dyadic pain might well be borne by the survivor (inasmuch as the decedent would have had no opportunity to experience any of it). In protracted dying—as occurs in most cases—the present pain and anguish involved in the frightening anticipation of being dead may well be sharper for the person than the pain suffered then and afterward by the survivor. The algebra of death's suffering is a complicated equation. But in suicide, the anguish of the survivor's bereavement is nearly always special: sharp, prolonged, and inimical.

Suicide is a personal and interpersonal disaster. The moment of a disaster's happening is its most dramatic. But it is not its only moment. A tragedy has its warnings and precursors—and it has its sequelae. There is much to be done after an earthquake, explosion, avalanche, tornado, fire, flood—or suicide. Postvention—the events that come after the dramatic event that gives the entire sequence its label—aims to mollify the inimical psychological sequelae in survivor–victims.

It is probably not an oversimplification to say that in our culture there are essentially two kinds of mourning and grief and reconstitutive patterns: (a) those that accrue to deaths from heart, cancer, accident, disaster, and the like, and (b) those that relate to the stigmatizing death of a loved one by suicide. I believe that the person who commits suicide puts his psychological skeleton in the survivor's emotional closet; he sentences the survivor to deal with many negative feelings and more, to become obsessed with thoughts regarding the survivor's own actual or possible role in having precipitated the suicidal act or having failed to stop it. It can be a heavy load.

We hear a great deal about suicide prevention and intervention. A benign community ought routinely to provide postventive health care for the survivor–victims of suicidal deaths. Postvention is prevention for the next decade and for the next generation. Of the three possible (temporal) approaches to mental health crises—prevention, intervention, and postvention—in the case of suicide at least, postvention probably represents the largest problem and thus represents the greatest area for potential aid. If there are about 50,000 committed suicides in the United States each year—not counting the couple of million "subintentioned" deaths presently labeled natural, accidental, and homicidal deaths—then there are at least 200,000 survivor–victims created each year whose lives are blighted by that event. A comprehensive understanding of "the suicidal problem" obviously ought to include postvention along with prevention and intervention in a tripartite approach.

Cain's volume, for the first time in explicit form, harnesses the neglected third horse of the troika; a beast that has been variously called *follow-up, sequelae,* or *aftermath.* Thus, his book rectifies an important error of historical omission in suicidology. I hope that it augurs a beginning of considerable focus on the tragedies that continue after the self-destructive deed—what I would call the *illegacy* of suicide.

Cain has assembled an especially interesting and stimulating set of writings, both obscure and well known, including some important catalytic papers of his own. I believe that clinicians and theorists will be stimulated and informed by his volume. As a practicing suicidologist, I welcome it.

SURVIVORS
OF
SUICIDE

Edited by

ALBERT C. CAIN, Ph.D.
Professor, Department of Psychology
University of Michigan
Ann Arbor, Michigan

With a Foreword by

Edwin S. Shneidman, Ph.D.
Professor of Medical Psychology
Department of Psychology
University of California at Los Angeles
Los Angeles, California

CHARLES C THOMAS · PUBLISHER
Springfield · Illinois · U.S.A.
[1972]

CONTENTS

158

PART IV. INDIVIDUAL CASE STUDIES

SURVIVORS OF SUICIDE

CHILDREN'S DISTURBED REACTIONS TO PARENT SUICIDE:
Distortions of Guilt, Communication, and Identification

. . .

PSYCHOLOGICAL IMPACT UPON CHILDREN OF SUICIDES

Proceeding beyond such indications of children's involvement in parental suicide, the study presented in this first section of the paper represents an initial clinical exploration of the psychological impact of parent suicide upon children. It is based on the case materials of forty-five *disturbed* children, all of whom had one parent who had committed suicide.* The children, ranging in age from four- to fourteen-years-old, had almost all been seen for diagnostic evaluation and/or treatment in child guidance

From *Survivors of Suicide* (pp. 93–100), by A. C. Cain (Ed.), 1972, Springfield, IL: Charles C Thomas. (Albert C. Cain & Irene Fast, authors). Copyright 1972 by Charles C Thomas. Reprinted with permission.

I picked this particular selection from Cain's book because it is about the effects of suicide on children, the most affected group of survivors, and I thought that this volume ought to have a piece about survivors, especially young ones.

*Note these were *all* disturbed children, permitting us minimal opportunity for studying more adaptive, integrative responses to parent suicide—and suggesting caution in the generalization of our findings.

settings. The materials of the study consisted of the typical data from out-patient evaluations (usually though not always including a developmental history, psychiatric interviews, diagnostic testing, and referral materials), plus therapy notes from outpatient treatment if initiated, and in nine cases the additional materials from inpatient treatment.

While the focus of this report will be upon some frequently encountered dimensions and patterns of disturbed reactions to parent suicide, each child's response, of course, was in important ways individual, embedded within his unique personality structure. Even the very suicidal acts themselves had quite distinctive features, each with its individualized impact upon the child.* It should also be clear that such data as school records, prior evaluations, and extended clinical contact demonstrated that the severe psychopathology found in these children is by no means to be traced solely to the direct impact of the parent suicide and the highly pathogenic chain of events it frequently sets in motion.

Lastly, these children each had to cope with many of the psychological stresses and burdens typical of parent loss: their surviving parent's shock, grief, preoccupied withdrawal, guilt, and blaming; their own heightened separation problems and deep sense of loss; misconceptions and fears of death; irrational guilts; anger over desertion; distorted intertwining of the bereavement reactions of the child and the surviving parent; realignments of family dynamics necessitated by the loss; stressful changes made in basic living arrangements; revival or heightening of intrapsychic conflicts and the related problems of the one-parent family (Neubauer). Insofar as possible the following observations are restricted to those relevant to parent *suicide as such*, rather than dealing with general characteristics of childhood bereavement (Arthur, Fast, Bowlby). Definitive assessment of the unique impact of parent suicide† will ultimately require supplementing such clinical qualitative investigations with quantitative comparative studies involving groups of children who have experienced different forms of parent loss.

The nature of this study's data—cases seen from a few days to more than ten years after the parent's suicide, at a number of clinics with different recording practices by various staff members, the clinical material (often from closed cases) ranging from brief diagnostic evaluations to detailed notes of intensive psychotherapy—permits little meaningful statis-

---

*For example, suicide after completely unsuspected criminal acts were uncovered and publicized, suicide in which the child's siblings were killed, suicide amidst a series of bereavements.

†Some of the differences in impact from other forms of bereavement are implicit in the very nature of the suicide's act: its abruptness, deliberateness, lack of inevitability; its implicit accusation and overt rejection of the suicide's objects; the virtual impossibility (by contrast with death from natural causes or accidents) of excluding psychic considerations and interpersonal events as causative factors; also, the unique stresses upon the bereaved following a suicide, and the community's tendency to avoid or blame rather than support the suicide's survivors.

tical analysis. In the sample there were thirty-two boys and thirteen girls, with approximately twice as many of the parent suicides being fathers as mothers. The age of the children at the time of the suicide: 15 percent under three years old; 30 percent between three and six years old; 40 percent between six and twelve years old; and 15 percent over twelve years old. The mean period between the parent suicide and psychiatric referral was slightly over four years. It is perhaps worth briefly noting that along a number of dimensions, this group of children was not appreciably different from one of the major clinic's general population in sex ratio, nature of referral sources, age at referral, or range of disorders.

The children ranged widely in the severity of their psychopathology, from relatively mild neurotic conditions to psychoses. What is most striking is that even with conservative diagnostic assessment, eleven of the forty-five children must be considered unquestionably psychotic (as compared with only four psychoses in a *roughly* comparable non-suicide group of forty-five childhood bereavement cases). Whether contrasted with childhood psychosis incidence figures from the general population or from the Children's Psychiatric Hospital where the majority of these children were seen, the incidence of psychotic conditions in this parent suicide group was many times that of the more general group of disturbed children—a tribute not only to the impact of the suicide but of course also to the pathological pre-suicide family background.

The symptom pictures of the children covered a broad spectrum, including psychosomatic disorders, learning disabilities, obesity, running away, tics, delinquency, sleepwalking, firesetting, fetishism, and encopresis, along with characterological problems, classical neurotic disorders and psychotic conditions. Perhaps the most meaningful division of these children into clinical subgroups would include two major groups, composing approximately 60 percent of the total sample: those children whose disorders were of a minimally veiled depressive nature—typically sad, guilt-laden, withdrawn, fearful, inhibited children—and those with more alloplastic object-loss reactions, especially seen in the more angry, truculent, defiant child, whose plentiful aggressive behavior often seemed poorly organized and almost objectless in nature.

. . .

Turning from a brief, necessarily sketchy characterization of the sample, this portion of the report deals exclusively with *two* crucial facets* of disturbed reactions to parent suicide: (1) the role of guilt and (2) distortions of communication. While the forms of these distortions varied con-

---

*A broader, more comprehensive study of such children will need in particular to focus upon such aspects of their object-relationships as their rage-filled sense of abandonment and desertion, their disillusionment, their distrust, their fear of and yet need to recreate tormenting situations of separation, the undertow-like pull toward identification with the suicided parent, and their defensive struggle against that identification.

siderably, dependent upon a myriad of factors (preexistent personality of child and surviving parent, nature of the suicide and the child's relationship to it, the child's age, etc.), their presence was pervasive and often quite blatant.

The child's guilts related to his parent's suicide were generally so intense that the superego distortions were readily visible in the child's psychopathology: overt in open, even insistent statements of guilt and self-recrimination, or prominent in a wide variety of pathological forms including depression, masochistic character formations, guilt-laden obsessive ideation, character structures based on rebellion against an externalized superego, rampant self-destructiveness, and reaction-formated suffocating passivity, inhibition, undoing, and ultra-goodness.*

Particularly striking were the multiple sources and foci of these guilts. In part, they inevitably derived from typical preexisting sources of hostile wishes toward the suicidal parent, these hostile impulses and fantasies being seen as fulfilled by and responsible for the parent's death. Such hostile wishes stemmed from customary sources in parent-child interaction, varied from totally unconscious to quite open anger and in some instances had been unfortunately heightened *just* prior to the suicide by otherwise transient resentments such as a refusal to give the child a two-wheeler bicycle. But quite aside from these typical sources of children's guilt in the face of parent loss, there were numerous special wellsprings. Where the parent's suicide was the outgrowth of a long-standing depressive character structure or condition, the depressive parent often had long exercised his expertise at making his children (as well as his spouse) feel guilty about and partially responsible for his sadness and despair—all the more so, then, for his suicide. Where the parent had been severely disturbed, especially in borderline or highly agitated conditions, often the child had been told, warned and scolded by his other parent or the family physician that he was "upsetting Mom," that he was "driving her crazy," that he must be very quiet, be very good, mustn't argue or upset her "even if she does do funny things sometimes," placing a large burden of responsibility on the child. Even more devastating were those cases where the parent's repeated histrionic suicide threats and gestures had eventually driven the frightened but increasingly exasperated child to the point of consciously angrily wishing that the parent would "go ahead and do it."

. . .

Aside from specific incidents prior to the suicide, the children often felt they were primarily responsible for the general background events and feelings that led to the suicide. That is, the child was convinced it was his

---

*Of course, the guilts stemming from the parent's suicide were not in vacuo experienced, defended against and transformed into symptomatology and/or character structure. The guilts were also displaced to other events or spheres, just as other and earlier guilts were fused, absorbed or hidden under the suicide-bred guilts.

basic badness or his father's disappointment in him that bred unhappiness and ultimately suicide; or he blamed himself for a good share of the marriage difficulties, for consistently siding against the suicidal parent in arguments, for "costing too much" amidst financial troubles, and he especially recalled parental arguments about himself.

Another constellation of guilts frequently encountered centered around the suicidal act. These children felt they should have stopped it, should have saved their parents somehow. Some plagued themselves with feeling it would not have happened if they had only been home instead of at camp or at the playground or at a friend's house. Others fiercely condemned themselves for not having told someone about previous suicidal attempts, or preparations for the suicide. In some instances the children had not initially understood what they saw of earlier attempts or preparations, or were too frightened to talk about them, or had been sworn to secrecy, or were rebuffed before when they tried to tell. Particularly guilt-inducing were those instances where the child had been asked to watch over a potentially suicidal parent, to "call daddy right away at the office if mommy seems real upset," or "make sure you watch and go with her if she goes down into the basement." This enormous burden was transformed into equally intense guilt when the child failed to warn of or stop the suicide. Similarly, some children found grounds for blaming themselves for not getting help soon enough—for not running quickly enough, not knowing who to call, not opening the windows or being able to drag their parent's body out of a gas-filled room. The ferocity of their guilt was fully evidenced by their absolute *insistence*—in the face of therapists' interpretations and reality confrontations—that it was their fault.

12

VARAH
THE SAMARITANS:
BEFRIENDING THE SUICIDAL

Originally published in London, 1973

The extraordinary motion picture "The King of Hearts" demonstrated effectively (and in the living color of powerful emotions) that the inmates could indeed take over the asylum—and run it much better. Nonetheless, by and large, the world remains hierarchical: Captains do not change insignia with corporals; police officers do not exchange places with fugitives and, above all, doctors do not trade gowns with patients. In relation to suicide prevention, until early in the 20th century in the United States, the big question was, What is the role (if any) of the nonprofessional volunteer in a professional enterprise?

Chad Varah, an Anglican clergyman in London, starting in 1953 developed a telephone service staffed almost entirely by volunteers "to befriend the suicidal and the despairing." Suffice it to say that in the past half century this enterprise has flourished and has become an international movement. At the turn of the 21st century, there are over 100 Samaritan branches—"The Samaritans" is the name chosen by Varah from the parable of Jesus—in Great Britain alone, not to mention branches in almost 80 countries around the world. The Samaritans are a distinctly British enterprise and a wonderfully successful one. They have a royal patron, HRH The Duchess of Kent, and Varah has been honored on the Queen's birthday list as an Officer of the British Empire.

Varah is the revered elder figure of the Samaritans. His books are the worldwide voice of volunteers in the suicide prevention enterprise. Somehow—for sociological reasons that are not too elusive (relating to the differences between Great Britain and the United States)—the movement did not catch on in America.

Nevertheless, at the first meeting of the American Association of Suicidology in Chicago in 1968, Louis I. Dublin, one of the grand old men of suicidology, said,

> The lay volunteer was probably the most important single discovery in the fifty year history of suicide prevention. Little progress was made until he came into the picture. The lay volunteer had the time and the qualities of character to prove that he cared. With proper training he can make a successful approach to the client, and by his knowledge of community resources available for useful referral he can often tide the client over his crisis. . . . It is essentially the story of the Samaritans of Britain, who in [a few] years, stretched the one-man experiences of Chad Varah into the [numerous] units now operating in virtually every large center of population in England and Scotland, involving thousands of dedicated volunteers and thousands of suicidal persons who come under their care.[1]

Two historic American threads come to my mind that are conceptually related to the Samaritans. The first is the Emmanuel Movement (1906–1910) in Boston (and throughout the United States), which had impeccable Bostonian credentials, that grew out of the friendship between some Episcopalian ministers and some Harvard Medical School physicians. It is an exciting and dramatic history told brilliantly in the 1998 book by Eric Caplan, *Mind Games: American Culture and the Birth of Psychotherapy*,[2] and in a 1998 article "Popularizing American Psychotherapy: The Emmanuel Movement, 1906–1910."[3] The "turf" was that new practice: psychotherapy. The two groups—ministers and doctors—got together with the quaint notion that ministers of the soul might also be ministers of the psyche; that laypeople (the clergy) could tend to nonsomatic emotional distress. Problem was, they could and did—with rousing public success. In the end, the

[1] Dublin, L. I. (1969). Suicide prevention. In E. Shneidman (Ed.), *On the nature of suicide* (pp. 45–46). San Francisco: Jossey-Bass.
[2] Caplan, E. (1998). *Mind games: American culture and the birth of psychotherapy*. Berkeley: University of California Press.
[3] Caplan, E. (1998). Popularizing American psychotherapy: The Emmanuel Movement, 1906–1910. *History of Psychology, 1*, 289–314.

physicians fell out with their clergy acquaintances—no longer dear colleagues—and had to take psychotherapy back for medicine, to require professional (i.e., medical) credentials to do "talk" therapy. Varah did not have this problem in Great Britain. Perhaps the Emmanuel Movement needed a royal sponsor.

Another American movement that comes to mind is Carl Rogers's nondirective therapy—first enunciated in the 1940s—that focused on reflecting the client's feelings and tried to steer away from psychodynamic interpretation or the giving of advice. The therapy was permissive, client centered (*Client-Centered Therapy*[4]). I could not find any reference to Rogers in any of Varah's books, but the parallels are obvious. In a recent newsletter of *Befrienders Worldwide*, a volunteer wrote,

> When I was a volunteer in the Hong Kong Centre, I first became aware of the immense isolation of those who called us. . . . I saw how sharing these painful moments with a Samaritan could alleviate their isolation and perhaps make the risk of suicide a little less immediate. . . . [A caller] wanted answers. What could we do? Listen, care and be there for him in the darkest moments of despair.

Words like *transference* and *countertransference* are not in their lexicon. They are not taboo; they are simply foreign. Samaritan responses may sound tepid (compared with depth psychotherapy), but their human power is that of a steamroller. From my personal observation, Varah himself is not especially nondirective by nature; he is filled with straightforward commonsense advice.

Varah is the consummate public relations man for suicide prevention. His office is the crypt—lined with ancient human bones—of St. Stephen's church in the center of old London. It is better than any movie setting; it is real.

Varah's series of books on the Samaritans is like a series of memoranda to the troops and to the public about the organization that he founded. Varah's books are important not only because, taken in their entirety, they are the field manual for an extensive organizational operation, but also because they are implicitly about a topic not often explicitly discussed, namely the role of the lay volunteer in dealing with suicidal persons in the community. "In the community" means people calling from their homes or public telephones. The use of the telephone—with all the special psychological advantages and problems it introduces—is an essential characteristic of the Samaritan operations.

Varah has done—put together, written and edited, revised—the

---

[4]Rogers, C. (1951). *Client-centered therapy*. Boston: Houghton-Mifflin.

basic Samaritan text a number of times, all published by Constable and Company of London: (a) *The Samaritans*; (b) *The Samaritans in the '70s: To Befriend the Suicidal and the Despairing*; (c) *Answers to Suicide: Twenty Questions Posed and Answered by Chad Varah*; (d) *The Samaritans in the '80s*; and (e) *The Samaritans: Befriending the Suicidal*. The message is clear: befriending; nurturing; freely giving the gift of presence and acceptance is the decent, humane (Christian, Jewish, Muslim, Buddhist, atheist) thing to do. Samaritans are carefully chosen and carefully trained. They are committed to doing random acts of kindness.

Varah himself is filled with straightforward, no-nonsense advice. Here is one paragraph, no different in tone from dozens of others:

> Between the fanatics who have the answers for everyone else, and the Samaritans who want to help people find their own answers, there is such a great gulf fixed that any attempt to cooperate would be a waste of time. Those who "know" that "Jesus is the answer" (whatever this may mean) before they heard the question, seem to Samaritans to be terribly insecure people using slogans to avoid facing the complexity of human existence; and doubtless they in their turn see Samaritan tolerance as indifference to sin, and Samaritan recognition of the goodness in all sorts and conditions of men to be apostasy. Between these two attitudes there is no fence to sit on and no compromise possible; the sharper the conflict, the clearer the issues, the more chance people have of choosing the side that really suits their character and outlook.[5]

Chad Varah is suicidology's most powerful practitioner. He is the patron saint of the suicide prevention volunteer. To read his books is a unique and uplifting experience and to meet him is a life-enhancing experience.

---

[5] Varah, C. (1985). *The Samaritans: Befriending the suicidal* (p. 36). London: Constable.

The Samaritans:
Befriending the suicidal

Edited and with an Introduction by

CHAD VARAH

Constable London
[1985]

CONTENTS

THE SAMARITANS

"What gave you the idea?"

For over thirty years people have been asking me this within a few minutes of meeting me. If there had been a simple answer, I should soon have got sick of hearing myself repeat it. But any answer attempting to be accurate would be far too long for a dinner table conversation or an interview with a journalist, let alone a television appearance where one may be required to deal with half a dozen questions in two and a quarter minutes; as will be evident when I try to explain the origin and ethos of The Samaritans in the following pages.

Years of attempting to reduce the length and complexity of the answer without distorting the facts have produced the following.

For as long as I can remember I have been a scientist, i.e., a person with a persistent curiosity about how and why, preferring facts to opinions and experiments to guesswork. So when I read in 1953 that there were three suicides a day in London, my restless mind busied itself with the question "Why?"

I knew nothing about suicide and unthinkingly accepted the view then prevalent that you had to be of unsound mind to commit it. So the

From *The Samaritans: Befriending the Suicidal* (pp. 17–27, inclusive), by Chad Varah (Ed.), 1985, London: Constable & Robinson. Copyright 1985. Reprinted with permission.
  I picked this particular selection from Varah's book because it is a lively personal account of how he got started and gives us a good feeling of the special Varah tone with which the Samaritans operated for years. Only a British iconoclastic clergyman might have pulled it off.

puzzle was, if these people were mentally ill, why didn't they go to their doctor? Our National Health Service was, and is, free. I made some enquiries and found that a majority of those who had killed themselves had visited their doctor within three weeks of their death. Obviously, enormously greater numbers had consulted their doctors and not killed themselves, so these three a day could just be the few failures; but it was also possible that at least some of them (plus some of those who hadn't been to their doctor) were not in fact people whose primary need was for medical treatment. But if not medicine or psychiatry, what did they need?

There was only one way to find out for sure; ask them. And there was only one obstacle: no one knew who they were until it was too late.

. . .

While on a busman's holiday at an English Church on the Belgian coast I received an invitation from the Worshipful Company of Grocers to apply for their living of St. Stephen Walbrook, Wren's masterpiece next door to the Mansion House.

What would I do there if they appointed me? I told them about my plan for trying to save people from suicide. The successful and intelligent men on the Court asked searching questions and then told me they had decided to appoint me because they thought the experiment worth trying.

I then went up and down the pubs of Fleet Street telling journalists (many of whom I knew through Marcus Morris and *Eagle*) what a "human interest" story I had for them, and thanks to them a good start was made towards the achievement by 1984 of 94% of adults knowing about what the *Daily Mirror* decided in 1953 to call a "Samaritan" service.

. . .

As the days and weeks went by, it became clear that there were far more callers (up or in) than two of us could cope with, and a growing mailbag as well, not to mention the journalists whom we never put off however busy we were, for without publicity our service would have ground to a halt. Fortunately, the newspaper stories were so appealingly written (even though our strict rule of total confidentiality deprived journalists of fascinating case histories) that in addition to people needing help they attracted people wanting to *give* help. These were of two kinds: professionals, who could be held in reserve, and "ordinary" people, whom we liked and invited to come regularly, or whom we had doubts about and sent away. Our instinct in this matter was sound but it was some weeks before we discovered what these volunteers could do when given the chance.

The First Samaritans

Those first volunteers, all of whom I still remember vividly, were humble-minded people who did not suppose for a moment that *they* could save lives, but who were kind-hearted enough to want to help *me* and imaginative enough to realise that from what they had read, I must have taken on an impossible job. They saw themselves as being like Lepidus, "meet to be sent on errands," and were ready to spend hours just giving tea or coffee and an attentive ear to the people who were waiting for the important thing, an interview with me. I am ashamed to say that at that time I fully concurred in their opinion of our relative merits as life-savers, but I've made up for it since.

In fact, it was only a few weeks before I began to suspect that the volunteers, who met every Monday lunchtime for instruction and whom I liked and admired more the more I saw of them, had a much more valuable function than to keep people from getting too impatient and agitated whilst waiting to see me. It was a straightforward matter of observation that the proportion of the callers I actually interviewed diminished, the ones I did see were easier to help because of the time they had spent with a volunteer, and on the whole the people they passed on to me were rightly judged to be in need of a kind of professional attention the volunteers could not give. Eventually I was seeing only about one in eight of those who came, and this proportion was later discovered to be the proportion who, in addition to what we were to call "befriending," needed counselling or psychotherapy, or referral for psychiatry or other medical treatment.

Of course, human nature being what it is there were some callers who insisted on seeing me and no one else even though they needed only to have someone listen sympathetically to their problems and could just as well have bent the ears of the volunteers—better, in fact, because I was run off my feet and they weren't. But I am glad now that I sometimes had the experience of being with a very distressed person who could have his or her situation transformed not by any of the techniques I was clever at, but by my shutting up and listening with full attention. It was harder for me than for the volunteers, because I *could* do something more impressive and they couldn't, but by being able to manage it with an effort I was the more ready to believe in the value of listening therapy as it slowly become clear that whatever they said, that was what most people really wanted and needed.

It was a great relief to realise that as the service became better known, I would not need to increase my workload to an impossible extent, nor would I need to recruit more than a few other people with similar qualifications to my own. All I would need to do would be to analyse what the best volunteers were doing and select as many more like them as possible and teach them skills which would come naturally to them. I began to eavesdrop whenever I had the opportunity, and also to question Vivien who could be in the same room without making the volunteers self-conscious, as she got on with typing the letters I had dictated whenever there was a moment to spare.

What *did* the volunteers do when they came to take their turn on duty? The answer seemed clear: A great deal of nothing. So what did they *say* when they attached themselves to some tearful or withdrawn or agitated caller? Their most frequent remarks seemed to be: Mmmmmmm. And: How sad. Oh, I *am* sorry. Not to mention: Won't you have another cup of coffee? And, when challenged by the caller: No, not at all—take your time. No, I've nothing else to do—this is what I'm here for. Or, when asked for advice: I wouldn't know what to advise. I'm not any sort of an expert. What do *you* feel would be best?

Their sympathy was human sympathy. I never asked them about their religious beliefs, but I gathered that not all were any kind of believer—not that it mattered, as those that were didn't talk about it. They seemed to know instinctively that any talk of the love of God might be taken as an excuse not to give their own love, and and suggestion of prayer might be regarded as a rebuke if the caller felt deserted by any God there might be. Naturally, this attitude was reinforced by what I said on the subject at our Monday meetings, and by their knowledge that I rejected people who offered to join us if I found them preachy or bossy or prone to give advice or prudish. In those days, my selection was by my own subjective standards and I made some mistakes (it's now objective and sophisticated). My team and I worked on the basis of mutual confidence, and I had looked searchingly into every volunteer's eyes and asked myself the question. If I had done something of which I was horribly ashamed, could I tell it to that face?

. . . I was happy to set their fears at rest. I told them that I would still be "the boss," still choose them, instruct them, discipline them, and if necessary sack them, would still see the people they were unable to help by their befriending alone, and still make all the decisions and all the referrals. In addition, I alone would deal with publicity, and I would still be the one to open the mail. Before long, we settled down into the new pattern. I have taken so much space in recalling these events of more than thirty years ago because they are still relevant. Wherever we exist in the world, we still stand or fall by the befriending, the listening therapy, performed by people who are chosen for their aptitude for that, and for nothing else whatsoever.

What I want to make clear is that The Samaritans are a precise tailor-made answer to a universal need in the lonely, anxious, depressed and suicidal. I did not ask what I wanted to give, but what the clients (as we then called them) wanted to receive. I did ask what I was capable of giving, and discovered that of the two things I could do, the one most in demand was the one that any Samaritan could do, and most could do better than I.

During the next five years, I learnt more about what carefully-selected and well-supervised Samaritans could do, and as their numbers increased I was able to be more and more "choosy" in turning down any applicants about whom I had any doubts. "We can't afford to give the benefit of the doubt to anyone who, if they aren't right for the job, may cost a client's life," was the way I put it, with the full backing of the Samaritans. Indeed, in those years, anyone I accepted was "on observation" by the tried-and-tested Samaritans before being confirmed as one of us. (They thought it meant they were to observe what went on, and of course they did that too, but the purpose of Observation Duty was so that *we* might observe *them*.)

In addition to becoming more selective about new applicants, I had an occasional purge of existing members. If I found that they were unreliable, unpunctual, or guilty of some fault which could be corrected, I gave them a second chance; but there was no second chance for behaviour which showed that the person wasn't a Samaritan at all. Such things as gossiping about clients' affairs or trying to convert a client to the volunteer's religion or philosophy or arranging secret meetings with a client outside the centre led to instant dismissal. . . .

. . .

Any human institution is liable to be corrupted because of the defects in human beings. Samaritans, being hand-picked, might be expected to be relatively immune, but unfortunately their very niceness makes them too tolerant of power-seekers, and their rather selfish desire to avoid boring administrative tasks and confine themselves to the heartwarming or heart-rending work with the callers gives opportunities to unscrupulous and non-Samaritan persons to obtain influence if once they can con their way in at all. In those early years we had what seemed to be the perfect answer: we elected to the Committee the most exemplary Samaritans we could find, overruling their protests, and never gave the slightest power to people who seemed to want it.

13

COLT
THE ENIGMA OF SUICIDE

Originally published in New York, 1991

George Howe Colt is a Harvard University graduate and has an advanced degree from Johns Hopkins University. He is a working journalist. He is also a published poet and playwright. And, like the doctor-in-spite-of-himself, he is a social critic and student of his times. His 1991 book, *The Enigma of Suicide*, is not advertently a historiographic study of the United States in the 1960s, 1970s, and 1980s, but that is what, in the end, it turns out to be. Like Arthur C. Inman's diary, it is the story of a third of the 20th-century pie, essentially the Kennedy–Johnson–Nixon era of American life. Colt's fact-packed book—the facts of who was doing what—does not in its extensive index list the names of any of these three presidents, but their faces are omnipresent in the background of the murals of the period that he paints.

Suicide—unspokenly defined as a malady and a tragedy to be contained and its incidence reduced—and suicide prevention cannot be understood apart from this background. Colt brings this era to life through a series of journalistically brilliant vignettes and anecdotes about suicide and the suicide prevention movement. That movement, Colt implies, was given its realistic permissiveness by the *zeitgeist* and the beneficent attitudes toward mental health and large government programs of the Kennedy and Johnson administrations.

It is my observation that it is a fact of political life that more conservative national administrations, as they affect mental health programs, tend to be more biologically oriented—and in my opinion more subtly moralistic and more punitive—than do more liberal administrations. For me, Colt's exciting book, without being overtly political, brings that era alive. It is an historical record of those times, seen, of all things, through suicidological eyes.

But Colt's book is about suicide, and it reflects an almost decade of intensive research, from 1983 to 1990, interviewing hundreds of suicidal and nonsuicidal people. Of all of the entries in this volume, it is perhaps the most accessible book for the average literate citizen who wants, in a single, easily readable book, an introduction to the whole field. In short, it is an informative book written by a layperson for the lay reader with which to enter the enigmatic world of suicidology. I could not leave it out.

THE
ENIGMA
OF
SUICIDE

———◆———

George Howe Colt

SUMMIT BOOKS

NEW YORK   LONDON   TORONTO   SYDNEY   TOKYO   SINGAPORE

[1991]

181

CONTENTS

THE ENIGMA OF SUICIDE

SOCIAL STUDIES

One August day in 1937, H. B. Wobber, a forty-nine-year-old barge-man, took a bus to the Golden Gate Bridge, paid his way through the pedestrian turnstile, and began to walk across the mile-long span. He was accompanied by a tourist he had met on the bus, Professor Lewis Neylor of Trinity College in Connecticut. They had strolled across the bridge, which stretches in a single arch from San Francisco to the hills of Marin County, and were on their way back when Wobber tossed his coat and vest to Professor Neylor. "This is where I get off," he said quietly. "I'm going to jump." As Wobber climbed over the four-foot railing, the professor managed to grab his belt, but Wobber pulled free and leaped to his death.

Less than three months after the Golden Gate Bridge had opened to great fanfare, Wobber became its first known suicide. Since then more than eight hundred others have jumped, making it, as one researcher observes, "the number one location for suicide in the entire Western world." Ex-

From *The Enigma of Suicide* (pp. 329–331), by G. Howe Colt, 1991, New York: Summit Books. Copyright 1991 by George Howe Colt. Reprinted with permission of The Free Press, a division of Simon & Schuster, Inc.

I picked this particular selection from Colt's book because it illustrates the ambivalence, the indifference, and the active and passive hostility that face suicide and the people who attempt or commit suicide, even today. Along with the enigma of suicide, there is a mystique of suicide, which is not always on the side of suicide prevention.

cepting mass suicides like Masada and Jonestown, more people have chosen to end their lives at the Golden Gate Bridge than at any other location outside of Japan. As with most suicide statistics, the numbers are conservative. Only those who have been seen jumping or whose bodies are recovered are counted as bridge suicides. One expert suggests that more than two hundred others may have leaped unseen, in darkness, rain, or fog, been swept out to sea, and their bodies never found. A leap from the bridge is easy, quick, and lethal; one merely steps over a chest-high railing. At 70 to 85 miles per hour, the 240-foot fall lasts four seconds. If the force of the fall doesn't kill the jumper instantly, the fierce current will sweep him out to sea, to drown or be devoured by sharks. Of more than eight hundred people known to have fallen or jumped from the bridge since it opened, only nineteen have survived.

The Golden Gate Bridge is not the first location to exert a particular fascination for suicidal people. Throughout history certain cliffs, churches, and skyscrapers have earned reputations as suicide landmarks: Niagara Falls, the Cathedral at Milan, St. Peter's, the Eiffel Tower, the Empire State Building, and Giotto's Campanile on the Duomo in Florence are among them. Not all settings are grand. In 1813 in a French village a woman hanged herself from a large tree; within a short time several other women followed her example, using the same branch. In New York's Bowery there was a saloon in whose back room so many vagrants killed themselves, it became known as "Suicide Hall." And, of course, most towns have their "lover's leap." In Japan, where self-destruction has enjoyed institutional acceptance, many suicides choose spectacular natural settings for their deaths—"almost any place in Japan that is famous for its scenery is also famous for its suicides," observed an American visitor in 1930. Today, the country's leading suicide spot is Aokigahara-jukai, a dense forest at the foot of Mount Fuji, where about thirty people a year take their lives, usually by hanging or overdose, many of them coming from far away. A study of 116 people who attempted suicide in Jukai found that many believed the forest to be "a sanctuary where suicide was allowed," a setting that would "purify," or "beautify" their death.

Japan is also the setting for the most powerful magnet of all time, Mihara-Yama, a volcano on the island of Oshima, about sixty miles from Tokyo. On January 7, 1933, Mieko Ueki, twenty-four, and Masako Tomita, twenty-one, classmates at an exclusive Tokyo school, bought tickets on the small steamship that made three trips weekly to the island. After the six-hour passage the young women scaled the three-thousand-foot peak. When they reached the crater, which boiled and sputtered with sulfur clouds, Mieko told Masako that she had visited Mount Mihara the previous year and had been enchanted by the legend decreeing that the bodies of those who jumped into the crater were instantly cremated and sent to heaven in the form of smoke. This was a beautiful, poetic form of death, said

Mieko, and she intended to jump. Masako protested but eventually agreed not to intervene. The two girls bowed to each other. Then Mieko leapt into the smoking crater.

The story of the maiden and the volcano quickly became legend. Japan was in the midst of an economic depression, and the volcano became a national attraction for both tourists and suicides. In the remaining months of 1933, 143 people followed Mieko's example; on one April day there were six suicides, while twenty-five more were forcibly prevented. The deaths kindled a mixture of fascination and horror. The steamship company bought two new ships and made daily trips to accommodate the tourist flow; company shareholders made a profit on their investment for the first time in four years. Along the harbor fourteen hotels, twenty restaurants, and five taxicab companies opened within two years; the number of island photographers increased from two to forty-seven; a post office was built at the crater's edge; three camels were imported to carry tourists across the mile-wide strip of volcanic desert that surrounded the crater; horses ferried them to the summit. And a twelve-hundred-foot "shoot the chute" was built to spice up the return trip down the slope for those who chose to make it. Suicide had become a spectator sport; on a day when several hours had passed without a death, a tourist laughingly shouted, "I dare someone to jump!" A man ran forward and threw himself into the crater.

Eventually, the embarrassed government intervened. It was made a criminal offense to purchase a one-way ticket to Oshima, and plainclothes detectives were instructed to mingle with passengers on the boat, arresting anyone who looked bent on self-destruction—their criteria are not known. Tokyo police patrolled the crater; by the end of 1934 policemen and civilian onlookers had restrained 1,208 people from jumping. A barbed-wire fence was erected and a twenty-four-hour watch was posted. The hastily formed Mt. Mihara Anti-Suicide League even devised an elaborate arrangement of mirrors to give would-be suicides a terrifying view of the volcano's interior. Despite these efforts at least 167 more men and women leaped to their death in 1934, and 29 who had been restrained dove off the steamship returning them to Tokyo. By the time access to the mountain was closed in 1935, an estimated 804 males and 140 females had found their death in the volcano.

Although the authorities acted tardily in the case of Mount Mihara, elsewhere, when certain locations seem to beckon the suicidal, steps have been taken to discourage them. In 1850, an American physician traveling in Europe wrote: "At one time there seemed to be a growing propensity to jump from the Leaning Tower at Pisa; three persons—as I learnt from my guide while on a visit to it—having thus put a period to their existence; on which account visitors could no longer ascend it without an authorized attendant." In 1881 the column in Paris's Place Vendôme was closed following a wave of suicides. In the early twentieth century a lake near Kobe,

Japan, was drained because of the number of people who drowned themselves in its waters. Fences and barriers have greatly reduced the number of suicides at St. Peter's, the Eiffel Tower, and the Arroyo Seco Bridge in Pasadena. In the first sixteen years after the Empire State Building opened in 1931, sixteen people jumped to their deaths; not until 1947, when a man landed on a woman in the street below, critically injuring her, was a seven-foot spiked fence installed around the eighty-sixth-floor observation tower. In the next four decades only fourteen people jumped. In many other instances in which barriers, window stops, or emergency phones have been installed, suicides have been eliminated or greatly reduced. Nevertheless, despite more than eight hundred deaths and five decades of debate, no barrier has been erected at the Golden Gate Bridge.

Even before H. B. Wobber leaped to his death, there was concern about the Golden Gate's potential for suicides. Although the bridge was designed to accommodate benches for pedestrians, the bridge's board of directors feared they might be used as stiles, making it even easier for people to climb over the rail. The benches were never installed. Over the years, as the death toll mounted, various measures were considered: electric fences, barbed wire, safety nets, a twenty-four-hour motorcycle patrol, signs advising "Think Before You Leap," and legislation prohibiting jumping from the bridge. As early as 1953 a barrier was proposed. An engineer told the bridge board that the existing railing could be raised to seven feet for $200,000. All of these proposals were rejected as being either too expensive, too dangerous to workers on the bridge, too foolish, or merely ineffective.

In the face of increased publicity and rising public concern, a few precautions were taken. In 1960 the bridge board ordered pedestrian sidewalks closed between sunset and sunrise. By 1970 a closed circuit television system had been installed in the toll office, enabling workers to scan the pedestrian walkway and dispatch officers to restrain possible jumpers. A two-man tow truck roved the bridge. Patrolmen were taught to be on the lookout for women without purses, people edging away from their tourist group, or people staring intently at the surface of the water. Bridge personnel were trained in suicide prevention by a local prevention center. Over the years bridge workers, patrolmen, toll officers, passing motorists, and pedestrians have talked down or pulled back hundreds of would-be jumpers, often at risk to their own lives. One state highway patrolman assigned to the bridge claimed to have prevented 217 suicides in nine years on the job. Indeed, it is estimated that for every suicide from the bridge, two others are prevented.

During the suicide prevention movement of the late sixties and early seventies, the debate over an antisuicide fence came to a head. A committee was formed to lobby for a barrier, and a debate raged in editorials and letters to the editor. The bridge battle was a microcosm of debates about personal freedom and the value of life that have taken place around the country wherever antisuicide barriers have been proposed. How far should we go to prevent suicide? Bridge directors received hundreds of letters, about two-thirds opposing the barrier. Some argued that it would spoil the view: Why destroy the view for so many for the sake of so few? Others felt it was a waste of money: Why spend money on someone who wants to die? Others felt the money would be better spent on free mental health care. Many defended a person's right to suicide. "If and when I decide to die I would prefer the bridge as an exit point and I don't want to be kept from it by a high, jail-like railing," one woman wrote to the *San Francisco Chronicle*. "There are worse things than death and one should be able to make that personal choice if necessary." A few even argued that an unfettered bridge saved lives by acting as a magnet to which disturbed people were drawn and could be more easily intercepted and delivered to treatment. The most popular argument against a barrier was that it simply wouldn't work; common sense said that suicidal people would simply go kill themselves somewhere else.

Arguing in favor of the barrier, suicidologists pointed out that suicide is often an impulsive act, and the impulse, once thwarted, is frequently abandoned. They cited studies showing that only 10 percent of those who attempt suicide go on to kill themselves. They pointed to the fact that 90 percent of bridge suicides jump from the side of the bridge facing San Francisco—facing what they're leaving behind—as an indication of their ambivalence. They explained that suicidal people are apt to choose a highly personal method, and if that method is unavailable they may abandon their plans rather than switch to another. In a suicidal crisis, people often lack the flexibility to generate alternatives when foiled. The suicidologists pointed to other locales in which barriers had decreased the number of suicides without spoiling the view. They indicated that the lethality of the bridge and the impulsiveness of many suicides made the bridge an especially deadly combination. "The bridge is like having a loaded gun around," said psychiatrist Jerome Motto at a 1971 hearing. "I think it is the responsibility of those in control to unload the gun." Although the bridge board authorized a $20,000 preliminary study and a sample of the winning design was constructed, the debate dragged on and the barrier went unbuilt.

Then Richard Seiden, a pro-barrier Berkeley psychologist, gathered the names of 515 people who had been restrained from jumping from the bridge dating back to its opening day. Checking their names against death certificates he learned that only twenty-five had gone on to take their own lives. Although his research proved that people did not inexorably go on to commit suicide using another method, critics argued that people restrained from jumping were not truly bent on death. What about those who had jumped and lived? In 1975 psychiatrist David Rosen interviewed six of the eight people known to have survived leaps from the Golden Gate Bridge. None of the eight survivors had gone on to kill themselves; the six he interviewed all favored the construction of an antisuicide fence. They all said that had there been a barrier, they would not have tried to kill themselves some other way. Their plans had involved only the Golden Gate Bridge; like those who attempted suicide in the forest of Jukai, they spoke of an association between its beauty and death. For them, Rosen said, the bridge was a "suicide shrine."

A second study by Seiden supported the notion that the Golden Gate Bridge had a "fatal mystique." Comparing Golden Gate suicides to San Francisco–Oakland Bay Bridge suicides, he found that although the two spans were completed within a few months of each other and are about the same height, five times as many people had committed suicide from the Golden Gate Bridge as from the Bay Bridge. Unlike the Golden Gate, the Bay Bridge does not allow pedestrian traffic. Yet even when pedestrian suicides were omitted, the Golden Gate still spawned three times as many suicides. The Golden Gate Bridge, said Seiden, had become a "suicide mecca"; while its suicides usually made the front page, Bay Bridge suicides were rarely publicized. Seiden found "a commonly held attitude that often romanticizes suicide from the Golden Gate Bridge in such terms as 'aesthetically pleasing,' and 'beautiful,' while regarding Bay Bridge suicide as 'tacky' and 'déclassé.'" His statistics supported this: Half of the bridge suicides who lived east of San Francisco had chosen to drive over the Bay Bridge and across the city to the Golden Gate Bridge to end their lives.

Although Seiden's and Rosen's research seemed to put to rest the notion that if people were kept from killing themselves at the bridge, they would simply "go someplace else," the campaign for a barrier became a moot political issue. "The bottom line is money," says Seiden. "If it costs money, the bridge directors don't want to do it." (Today, a barrier would cost several million dollars.) Seiden also believes that San Franciscans like to think of their city as a tough-living, hard-drinking town and may take a perverse pride in the bridge's reputation. Gray Line tour bus drivers recite the bridge's suicide statistics in their tourist litany; guidebooks describe its fatal allure. The city's newspapers keep a kind of running box score in which news of each new jumper concludes with the observation that it is the bridge's nth suicide. In 1981 there was even a lottery in which players bet on the day of the week when the next Golden Gate suicide would take place.

Meanwhile, the suicides quietly continue. When Seiden sends out his research papers, he pencils in the updated statistics—from six hundred to seven hundred to "more than eight hundred." By 1990 there had been 885 confirmed deaths, including a depressed man who wrote in his suicide note, before stepping over the railing and leaping to his death, "Why do you make it so easy?"

One breezy autumn morning Seiden and I drove from downtown San Francisco toward the Golden Gate Bridge. Just before the toll booths on the bridge's south side he directed me onto a narrow road on the right marked "Restricted Access." About fifty yards down the road there was a deserted, weedy lot littered with ladders, broken window casings, and confusions of chicken wire. In the midst of this, like an abandoned sculpture, stood a curious metal structure, an eighteen-foot section of steel fence painted the same russet red as the Golden Gate Bridge. Its pencil-thin spires rose about eight feet into the air. On one half of the fence the spires pointed toward the sky; on the other half they curved gently inward at the top, like the fingers of a cupped hand. Through the graceful spires there was a stunning view of the Golden Gate Bridge as it leaped more than a mile over the bay into the soft green hills of Marin County. "Winning design number sixteen," said Seiden quietly. "It's been sitting here for years."

Bridge barriers, nets on observation decks, signs and emergency telephones on bridges, windows that don't open wide—these are only some of the ways in which "environmental risk reduction," as Seiden calls it, might help prevent suicide. "There is more than one approach to suicide prevention," says Seiden. "You can try to get inside people's heads and work with their self-esteem. You can work with parenting and with early recognition of depression, but you can also try to do something about the lethal agents of suicide—the guns, the pills, the bridges. It's the same as automobile safety. You can do driver training and you can make the car safer. You can change the environment as well as change the individual." With suicide seen almost exclusively from the medical model, however, the possibilities of environmental and social change have been all but ignored. Critics say that these are superficial measures, that Seiden is treating symptoms, not causes. "Sometimes that's all you can treat," says Seiden. "Frankly, we haven't had a good record in treating suicidal patients from the inside out."

For many years the most popular method of suicide in Great Britain was asphyxiation—sticking one's head in the oven and turning on the gas. After the discovery of oil and natural gas deposits in the North Sea in the fifties and sixties, most English homes converted from coke gas, whose high carbon monoxide content made it highly lethal, to less toxic natural gas. From 1963 to 1978 the number of English suicides by gas dropped from 2,368 to eleven, and the country's overall suicide rate decreased by one-third. Despite England's increasing unemployment and deteriorating race relations, it has remained at that lower level ever since. "If you could prescribe a situation that is tailor-made for suicide, England would be it," says Seiden. "Yet their rate is down 33 percent. Why? Because a highly lethal method has been taken away."

One area Seiden and other suicidologists are exploring is the link between the misuse of prescription drugs and suicide. British and Australian studies show that restrictions on prescribing barbiturates reduced the number of actual or attempted barbiturate suicides without increasing the number of suicides by other methods. Suicidologists have called for tighter regulation of potentially lethal medication and for training of physicians and pharmacists in clues to depression and suicide. They propose the use of blister packs, which require single capsules to be punched out individually, allowing more time for emotions to cool or rescuers to intervene.

"Much could be gained if we tried to make suicide more difficult for the potential candidate. . . . Opportunity makes the suicide as well as the thief," observed David Oppenheim at the 1910 meeting of the Vienna Psychoanalytic Society devoted to suicide. "An opportunity for self-destruction is offered to anyone who is in the position to bring about his death by some swift and easy action that is painless and avoids revolting mutilations and disfigurement. A loaded pistol complies so well with all these conditions that its possession positively urges the idea of suicide on its owner." Far more urging takes place now than in Oppenheim's day. There are an estimated 200 million civilian-owned guns in the United States, including some 60 million handguns. In the late 1960s a new handgun was sold every twenty-four seconds; in 1984 a new handgun was sold every twelve seconds. While numerous studies have linked increased gun ownership to increased rates of crime, armed robbery, and homicide, few have examined its effect on suicide.

Among all the countries in the world, only in the United States are guns the primary means of suicide. In a 1983 study, NIMH researcher Jeffrey Boyd scrutinized suicide rates for 1953 to 1978 and found that the firearm suicide rate had risen steadily while the rate by all other methods had declined. In 1953 firearm suicides accounted for 45.7 percent of all suicides; in 1978 they constituted 56 percent. The jump in firearm suicides accounted for an overall increase in the suicide rate from 12.4 in 1953 to 13.3 in 1978. Suggesting that the increase in suicide by firearms was related to the increase in gun sales and noting that handguns account for 83 percent of all suicides by firearms, Boyd concluded, "It is conceivable that the rise in the suicide rate might be controlled by restricting the sale of handguns."

Other research supports this hypothesis. A 1980 study found that the strictness of state gun-control laws was significantly correlated with suicide rates; in general, states with the toughest gun control laws had the lowest suicide rates. The rates in the ten states with the weakest handgun laws were more than twice as high as rates in the ten states with the strongest laws. A study of Los Angeles and California suicides during a three-year period in the mid-seventies found that citywide, countywide, and statewide the suicide rate by firearms rose and fell in near-perfect harmony with the volume of gun sales. "If guns are outlawed, only outlaws will have guns," a favorite National Rifle Association homily, implies that ordinary citizens need guns to protect themselves. Yet a handgun around the house is six times more likely to kill a family member than a burglar. In a study of eighty-two consecutive suicides in Cuyahoga County, Ohio, thirty-five were by gunshot. Only three of the guns had been purchased for the purpose of self-destruction; the majority had been acquired to protect the family. In a 1986 study of firearm deaths in the home in King County, Washington, there were thirty-seven suicides for every self-protection homicide. The use of a gun makes any suicide attempt five times more likely to be fatal. "If some persons would use slower methods of self-destruction, some lives might be saved," concluded a National Violence Commission report. "The possibility that the presence [of firearms] is in some instances part of the causal chain that leads to an attempted suicide cannot be dismissed. With a depressed person, the knowledge of having a quick and effective way of ending his life might precipitate a suicide attempt on impulse."

Despite these studies, while therapists commonly advise families of suicidal patients to "get the guns out of the house," little has been done on a broad scale to reduce firearm suicides. At the least, suicidologists recommend an enforced waiting period between purchase of a gun and the right to possess it since the suicidal impulse might fade during that time. Twenty-two states have laws requiring such a waiting period. Nevertheless, while more Americans kill themselves with guns than are murdered with them every year, suicide is rarely mentioned by either side in the gun control debate. In an editorial accompanying Jeffrey Boyd's research in *The New England Journal of Medicine*, Dr. Richard Hudgens admitted, "It is unlikely that the suicidal use of guns will be an important factor in any eventual decision to limit their availability, for suicide is not high on the list of America's political concerns." When approached with the idea that the soaring firearm suicide rate justified a call for tighter gun control, a National Rifle Association spokesman responded, "The NRA is not for gearing laws to the weakest element of society."

This Darwinian reflection seems to speak to the heart of the question of how far we should go to help prevent suicide. Clearly, we cannot and should not make the world "suicide proof" nor our lives a twenty-four-hour suicide watch. Even if we could, suicides would of course still occur. But even if bridge barriers and gun control legislation were to have no effect on the suicide rate, there may be compelling reasons why such measures should nevertheless be taken. To put up or not put up a barrier says something about the way we feel about suicide and the suicidal.

I remember discussing the proposed Golden Gate Bridge barrier with a San Francisco friend. "Ninety-nine percent of us don't need it," she said. "Is it fair to ruin the view for the sake of a few? If they want to die so much, why not let them?" I found this attitude shared by many people.

Their view often seemed based less on respect for individual freedom than on ignorance of the psychodynamics of self-destruction and discomfort with the subject of suicide in general. Whatever their reasons, it troubled me that so many otherwise kindhearted people should object to preventive measures. For how far is it from this passing condoning to the chorus one sometimes hears when a crowd has gathered at the base of a tall building, to watch the weeping man on the ledge high above, shouting, "Jump, jump, jump"?

Fortunately, in answer to the voices who cry "Jump," there are many other voices that cry "Live"—not just the voices of family, friends, therapists, and prevention center volunteers but the voices of strangers. When the twenty-year-old manager of a Brooklyn clothing store began receiving telephone calls for a now-defunct suicide prevention hot line, he took time to listen to their problems. "They just start talking," he said. "I tell them they have the wrong number, but I ask them if I can help. . . . I believe in helping people out." When a twenty-six-year-old Austrian threatened to jump from the 446-foot steeple of St. Stephen's in Vienna, a thirty-four-year-old priest whose hobby is mountain climbing scaled the steeple and persuaded the man to descend. When an eighteen-year-old girl stood on the ledge of a seven-story building in Mexico City, threatening to jump, Ignacio Canedo, an eighteen-year-old Red Cross male nurse, inched out toward her. Canedo was tied to a long rope, held on the other end by a squad of firemen. "Don't come any nearer!" shouted the girl. "Don't, or I'll jump!" Canedo grabbed for her and missed. The girl screamed and jumped. Canedo jumped after her, caught her in midair, and locked his arms around her waist. They fell four floors before the rope snapped taut. Canedo's grip held, and he and the girl were hauled back to the roof. "I knew the rope would save me," said Canedo. "I prayed that it would be strong enough to support both of us." There are dozens of similar stories of potential suicides saved by strangers who instinctively reached out.

As a term project for "The Psychology of Death," a course taught by Edwin Shneidman at Harvard, one student placed an ad in the personals section of a local underground newspaper: "M 21 student gives self 3 weeks before popping pills for suicide. If you know any good reasons why I shouldn't, please write Box D-673." Within a month he had received 169 letters. While the majority were from the Boston area, others came from as far away as New York, Wisconsin, Kentucky, even Rio de Janeiro. They offered many reasons why he should stay alive. Some wrote of music, smiles, movies, sunny days, sandy beaches. Some quoted Rod McKuen, e.e. cummings, or Dylan Thomas. They suggested he spend time with others less fortunate than he; implored him to think of those he would leave behind; called him a coward and dared him to struggle and survive. Some referred him to a therapist. Others offered friendship, enclosing their phone number or their address. A few enclosed gifts: two joints of marijuana; an advanced calculus equation; a Linus doll; magazine clippings on the subject of kindness; a photo of apple blossoms with the message, "We're celebrating Apple Blossom Time." Some simply broke down in the middle of their letters and pleaded, "Don't," or "You just can't."

The student was not actually contemplating suicide, but the answers he received were real. Whether they might have persuaded someone truly suicidal to stay alive or not is impossible to say. But if the forces that lead someone to suicide are numerous, those forces that combine to prevent someone from killing himself may be equally complex; whether they be tricyclic antidepressants, a prevention center volunteer, a barrier on a bridge, a Linus doll, or the voice of a stranger saying, "I care." "There is no magic bullet that goes right to the heart of suicidality," says Robert Litman. "Many, many things together bring a person to suicide, and many, many things together prevent a suicide. But if you have, say, twenty suicidal things and you can relieve just one, leaving only nineteen, you're probably going to get a sense of improvement and a little more hopefulness. And if you can maybe relieve parts of two or three others and get it down to seventeen, to sixteen, you're going to get another little increment of hopefulness, and you're on your way."

Harry Warren, Jr., the second director of the National Save-A-Life League, used to tell the story of a young reporter who, after several years of success on small-town newspapers, went to New York, hoping to make it as a writer in the big city. Things went poorly. He was unable to get work. Alone and friendless, without money, convinced he was a failure, his thoughts turned to suicide. One rainy day he went to a bridge and leaned over, tempted to jump to his death.

"By a heroic effort he turned away," said Warren, "but still struggling with the thought, journeyed back downtown by an express subway train. The man next to him turned abruptly and asked, 'Does this train stop at Chambers Street?' Though a New Yorker of recent standing himself, the reporter knew that much about the city, 'Yes,' he said with a sudden, strange ardor, 'it does.'

"So trivial a thing as that—an ability to direct someone when he himself was a comparative stranger in town—served to re-establish his self-assurance at a critical time. He went to his room, changed into dry clothing, and went to work gathering material for a feature story he had started on a few days earlier and abandoned. This fellow turned out all right."

EPILOGUE

THIS I BELIEVE

In the 1940s and 1950s, the famous broadcast journalist Edward R. Murrow conducted a newspaper column called "This I Believe." Murrow asked celebrities of all stripes—politicos, tycoons, movie stars, athletes, intellectual leaders—to share (in no more than 500 words) their heartfelt beliefs with the American public. In due course, my special intellectual hero Henry A. Murray—athlete, soldier, physician, surgeon, biochemist, psychoanalyst, Melville scholar, Harvard professor, and pioneer personologist—was invited to contribute. Here are a few excerpts from his brief essay:

> I believe that the word "believe" is, in its various meanings, slippery as a snake, and, like the fabled snake, apt—in a bewildered age like ours—to lead us into evil, the evil of hypocrisy. . . .
>
> As for personal history, I confess to constant gratefulness for the belief-engendering delights of mutual love, friendship, nature, travel, literature, and the vocation of psychology. My faith in the potential value of psychology has never wavered. . . .
>
> I believe, of course, in the cardinal virtues of courage, charity, and dedication, and I am still trying to bring my Adam into line with them. But the reiteration of these verities is evidently not enough, since after more than two thousand years of earnest preaching, that large portion of the human race which appears, in its own eyes, most advanced in these respects is on the verge of proving itself an utter failure. . . .[1]

---

[1] Murray, H. A. (1954). This I believe. In E. R. Murrow (Ed.), *This I believe* (page number not available). New York: Simon & Schuster.

I believe all that. In this setting, my own beliefs, less encompassing and less elegantly cognized, are confined to suicidology. In 1985, in *Definition of Suicide*, I wrote, "Suicide is a multifaceted event and that biological, cultural, sociological, interpersonal, intrapsychic, logical, conscious and unconscious, and philosophic elements are present in various degrees in each suicidal event" (p. 202).[2] This notion—of the multidisciplinary nature of suicide—has become commonplace, a mantra for suicidologists. That definition in its rote recitation of suicide's multiplicity is becoming too simplistic. Perhaps it is time for me to reexamine it. I now tend to believe that A. Alvarez, English poet and critic (and himself experiencing a failed suicide), was closer to the essence of suicide—closer to the kind of comprehension of suicide that I am trying to pursue—when he wrote "As for suicide [it is] a terrible but utterly natural reaction to the strained, narrow, unnatural necessities we sometimes create for ourselves."[3]

Following Murray, I believe that no branch of knowledge can be more precise than its intrinsic subject matter will allow. I believe that we should eschew specious accuracy. I know that the current fetish is to have the appearance of precision—and the kudos and vast monies that often go with it—but that is not my style. Nowadays, the gambit used to make a field appear scientific is to redefine what is being discussed. The most flagrant current example is to convert the study of suicide, almost by sleight of hand, into a discussion of depression—two very different things. (One can lead a long unhappy life with depression, but acute suicidality is often quickly fatal.)

I believe that suicide is essentially a drama in the mind, where the suicidal drama is almost always driven by psychological pain, the pain of the negative emotions—what I call *psychache*. Psychache is at the dark heart of suicide; no psychache, no suicide.

In my view, suicide is not a Kraepelinian category; suicide is not a disease; suicide is not a special physiological state. Suicide is not like syphilis, pneumonia, anthrax, encephalitis. There is no coccus, virus, spirochete, cerebrospinal fluid level, demographic profile, psychodynamic episode, unconscious attitude toward one's own father, or genetic bullet that causes suicide. The internal mental drama relating to the pain of negative emotions (shame, guilt, revenge, hopelessness, etc.) is surrounded by a syllogism that sees only escape as the acceptable solution.

We need to give back to *introspection* the good name that it had before the 19th-century psychologists Wundt and Titchener ponderously trivialized it. Each suicide has its own unrepeatable anguish and special logic; the mischief lies in that innocent word "therefore," as in "therefore I must kill myself." All of these flawed syllogisms are built on inner seemingly

[2] Shneidman, E. (1985). *Definition of suicide* (p. 202). New York: Wiley.
[3] Alvarez, A. (1971). *The savage God* (p. 272). London: Weidenfeld & Nicolson.

logical premises stemming from that mind's private psychodynamic history. I am almost ready to believe that each suicide may be *sui generis*; that each suicide is almost idiosyncratic in its own pattern of frustrated psychological needs.

I believe that the principal source of elevated psychache is a nexus of frustrated or thwarted psychological needs. In my view, the best available explication of psychological needs is to be found in Murray's 1938 *Explorations in Personality*.[4] A list might include the need for achievement, affiliation, aggression, autonomy, counteraction, defendance, deference, dominance, exhibition, harm avoidance, inviolacy, nurturance, order, play, rejection, sentience, shame avoidance, succor, and understanding. In the clinical setting one should distinguish between that individual's nexus of *modal* psychological needs, with which that person habitually lives, and that individual's constellation of *vital* psychological needs that the individual is willing to die for.

My view is definitely mentalistic. I believe that suicide is a matter of the mind. The mind—that mysterious microtemporal substance-free "secretion" of a unique organ made up of billions of specialized cells, called *consciousness*—has a mind of its own; the main business of the mind is to mind its own business. When it comes to suicide—which is my main business—I am a 21st-century mentalist.

It is my belief that our best answers, as therapeutic suicidologists, cannot come from medicine or physiology, or group behavior or epidemiology or sociology, not from Kraepelin nor the *Diagnostic and Statistical Manual of Mental Disorders*, and certainly not from Smith-Kline Beecham.

I believe that the rule for saving a life in balance can, amazingly enough, be rather simply put: Reduce the inner pain. When that is done, then the inner-felt necessity to commit suicide becomes redefined, the mental pressure is lowered, and the person can choose to live.

I believe that, in large part, psychotherapy consists in helping the patient reconceptualize the can'ts, the won'ts, the absolutes, and the nonnegotiables of the patient's present firmly held positions; to widen the stubbornly fixed blinders of present perceptions; to think the unthinkable. In my view, there is a 20th-century example of just this topic. Over a half century ago, on August 14, 1945, Japanese Emperor Hirohito—in the first-ever address to his people—in his historic prescript of capitulation, ordered his loyal subjects to surrender. In a few brief sentences, the emperor touched on the two main antidotes to suicide: a generational sense of the future and a personal redefining of what is intolerable—the two key lacunae of any suicidal scenario. His words are arguably the most effective suicide prevention speech ever made. Here in part is what he said (trans-

---

[4]Murray, H. A. (1938). *Explorations in personality* (pp. 142–242). New York: Oxford University Press.

lated): "It is according to the dictates of time and fate that we have resolved to pave the way for a grand peace for all the generations to come by enduring the unendurable and suffering what is unsufferable."[5] Those few words saved thousands of lives.

That is the formula for surviving a suicidal crisis: To redefine what is intolerable as something that is barely tolerable after all. To continue to live, one must listen to the voice—the benign macrotemporal voice—of the life-oriented emperor of one's mind.

Further, I believe that there is another concept that is central to all this business. If pain is key to suicide, and if that pain is fueled by frustrated psychological needs, then, obviously, we must address the pain. Lower the pain and the person can choose to live. A substance or an agent (a benign individual acting as helper) that relieves pain is called an *anodyne*. (See de Quincy's great 19th-century book, *Confessions of an English Opium Eater*,[6] for a discussion of anodynes.) I call my therapy with suicidal persons (which addresses the frustrated vital psychological needs indicated in *that* particular case) *anodyne therapy*.

A few words about anodyne therapy are appropriate here. I believe that the goal of anodyne therapy need not be the cure of some putative mental disease but rather the mollification of the individual's undeniable psychological pain. Even though anodyne therapy focuses on the deleterious role of frustrated psychological needs, it nevertheless has a positive orientation in that it seeks to liberate the individual from narrow, truncating, unhealthy, life-endangering views of the "self." Its goals include a deeper look at the possible life-sustaining alternatives that keep an individual under the tent of life in the booming circus of individual existence.

I believe that anodyne therapy would, in nearly every case, have a special focus on the positive life-enhancing needs. These might include, for example, the individual's need for achievement (to strive and to tolerate), for affiliation (to relate to others), for endurance (to somehow live with pain), for generational needs (to conceive of a future), and for nurturance (to help and sustain others). The exploration of an individual's frustrated psychological needs can be done, in the therapeutic setting, in a way that is neither hortatory nor pedantic.

I tentatively believe—guided by my own clinical experience—that for most practical purposes a majority of suicide cases tend to fall into one of four clusters of frustrated psychological needs. They exhibit themselves in different kinds of psychological pain.

1. *Thwarted love, acceptance, or belonging*—related primarily to the frustrated needs for succor and affiliation.

---

[5] Hanson, H. A., Herndon, G. C., & Langsdorf, W. G. (Eds.). (1947). *Fighting for freedom. Historic documents* (p. 135). Philadelphia: John C. Winston.
[6] DeQuincy, T. (1821, September–October). *Confessions of an English opium eater. London Magazine*, pp. 293–312, 353–379.

2. *Fractured control, excessive helplessness, and frustration*—related primarily to the frustrated needs for achievement, autonomy, counteraction, inviolacy, order, and understanding.
3. *Assaulted self-image and avoidance of shame, defeat, humiliation, and disgrace*—related primarily to the frustrated needs for affiliation, autonomy, defendance, shame avoidance, and succor.
4. *Ruptured key relationships and attendant grief and bereftness*—related primarily to the frustrated needs for affiliation and nurturance.

Of course, I believe that there are more than four kinds of suicide and that each sad case should be assessed, understood, and treated in its own idiosyncratic psychological terms.

Ruefully, I believe that practically all of the past and all of the current studies of suicide—demographic, psychiatric, psychoanalytic, or biological—have been ancillary; on the same field as the archery easel but not on the target, and nowhere near the bull's-eye. One needs to examine the problem of suicide with an open mind and a fresh template. What is critical is the reduction of that individual's psychache, itself created by unfulfilled psychological needs. I strongly believe that what is sensibly required is a therapeutic agent (person) who can reduce the perturbed individual's pain; in other words, an anodyne.

Regrettably, I believe that all of the demographic studies from Enrico Morselli (through Emile Durkheim, Maurice Halbwachs—19th century European "suicidologists"—and this year's dissertations) on; all the biochemical work, through the elegant laboratory experiments; all the important psychological and psychiatric papers cited by Maltsberger and Goldblatt (my own included); all the poignant confessionals about manic–depressive disorder are, at their best, background hum or music. But music, hum, or noise, they are background. They fail to address the necessary cause of suicide—as opposed to their focus on different kinds of perturbations (e.g., depression) or concomitants of suicide (e.g., social status or biochemical markers). For me, today, still, the core data to elicit from a potentially suicidal person are not a family history, a spinal tap assay, a demographic survey, a psychiatric account, a psychodynamic interview, or a self-report of a mental illness, but rather—keeping all of these relevant bits of information in mind—what is directly to the suicidal person's point, namely a full anamnestic response to the two basic questions in clinical suicidology: "Where do you hurt?" and "How may I help you?"

AUTHOR INDEX

SUBJECT INDEX

cal aspects of suicide; Significant others, impact on

Fences, 187–191

Fight, 138

Flight, 108, 111–122, 138

Fluoxetine (Prozac), 148

Focal suicide, 91, 93, 96

Follow-up. *See* Consequences of suicide; Postvention; Significant others, impact on

Freight, 138

Freud, Sigmund, 7–8, 51, 89, 90, 98, 119, 136, 142, 146

Fright, 138

Frigidity, 96

Galileo, 22

Games, 105, 108, 182

Gender, 44, 45–47, 54, 64, 108

Generational needs, 202

Genetics, 38, 77, 136

Goldblatt, Mark J., 135–139, 141–150

Golden Gate Bridge, 185–186, 188–191, 193–194

Greece, classical, 5, 54, 182

Grief, 108, 154, 158, 172

See also Significant others, impact on

Guilt, 159, 161–165

Halbwachs, Maurice, 7, 203

Handguns, 192

Harvard University, "Psychology of Death" course at, 194–195

Heredity. *See* Genetics

History of suicide, 5–9, 50, 54, 182

History of Suicide (Minois), 5, 6, 13–15, 17–22

Homo Ludens: A Study of the Play Element in Culture (Huizinga), 105

Hopelessness, 143

Hospice, 172

Hostility, 7–8, 143

HPA axis. *See* hypothalamic-pituitary-adrenal axis

Hudgens, Richard, 193

Hume, David, 6, 14–15, 20

Hypothalamic-pituitary-adrenal (HPA) axis, 76, 80–81

Iga, Mamoru, 59–61, 63–68

Illegacy of suicide, 155

Impotence, 96

Incest, 172

Individual as locus of blame, 5–6, 7–8

See also Freud, Sigmund; *The Inman Diary: A Public and Private Confession;* Sin

Inman, Arthur Crew, 123–126, 127–133

The Inman Diary: A Public and Private Confession (Aaron, ed.), 123–126, 127–133

Institutionalized suicide, 109

International Association of Suicide Prevention (Athens, 1996), 72

Interventions. *See* Treatment

Introspection, 200–201

In vivo imaging studies, 77

James, William, 50–51, 126

Japan

culture of, 59–68

popular settings for suicide in, 186–187

Jews, 54

Jones, Ernest, 136

Karpinos, Bernard D., 56–57

Ker, Sir Robert, 20

LASPC. *See* Los Angeles Suicide Prevention Center

Law, 54

Leaning Tower of Pisa, 187

Lindemann, Erich, 153

Listening therapy, 175–176

Literature, suicide and, 24, 26

See also Writers, suicides by

Lithium maintenance, 77

Litman, Robert E., 8, 195

Locus coeruleus, 77

"Longing to die," 142

Los Angeles Suicide Prevention Center (LASPC), 147

Ludic suicide, 104, 105, 108–109

Malingering, 96

Primate studies, 76
Primitive peoples, 54, 182
Problems, suicide as solution to, 104, 106, 121
Prozac, 148
Psychache, 144, 200–201, 203
Psyche, 8
Psychiatric inpatients, 144
Psychoanalysis, contemporary, 7–8, 142
    See also Menninger, Karl A.
Psychodynamic theory, 50, 61, 136, 137
Psychological aspects of suicide, 50, 54, 138
    See also Individual as locus of blame
Psychological needs, 201, 202–203
Psychological pain, 126, 139, 200–201, 202
Psychological resynthesis, 159
Psychological states, 38
Psychopathic states, 38
Psychopharmacology. See Anti-depressant drugs; Medication
Psychosis, 96
Psychosomatic medicine, 93
Psychotherapy
    See also Treatment
    nondirective, 169
    prevention and, 169, 201–202
    Samaritans and, 169
    transference and, 137, 143
    treatment and, 143
Punishment, 108
Purposive accidents, 96, 97–101

Race, 38
Reason, law of, 21
Rehabilitation of suicide, 19
Religious affiliation, 54
    See also Christianity; Jews
Renaissance, 14, 18, 26, 182
Rescue fantasies, 142
Right to die, 183
Risk assessment, 172
    See also Prediction of suicide
Rogers, Carl, 169
Romantic era, 26
Romantic suicide, 18
Rome, ancient, 54, 182
Romeo and Juliet, 99
Rosen, David, 189–190
Rousseau, Jean Jacques, 14, 15

Roy, Alec, 71–72

Sacrifice, 108
    See also Martyrdom
Sacrilege, 8
Saint-Cyran, Abbé de, 20
The Samaritans: Befriending the Suicidal (Varah, ed.), 167–170, 171–177
The Savage God (Alvarez), 23–30
Schizophrenia, 143
Scholarly approach, 13
    See also Dublin, Louis I.
Seasonal effects, 54
Seiden, Richard, 189, 190–192
Self-destructive behaviors, range of, 182
Selfhood, 8, 202
Self-mutilation, 96, 143
Seneca, 27
Sequelae. See Consequences of suicide; Postvention; Significant others, impact on
Serotonin, 76, 77, 81–82
Serum, 8
Setting. See Environment of suicide; Popular locations
Shakespeare, William. See Romeo and Juliet
Significant others, impact on, 183
    postvention and, 153–155
    Survivors of Suicide (Cain), 155, 157–165
Silverman, Morton, 72
Sin, 5–6, 8–9, 14, 20–21, 24, 182
    See also Individual as locus of blame
Society as locus of blame, 6–7, 14–15, 35, 38, 65, 191
    See also Colt, George Howe; Dublin, Louis I.; Durkheim, Emile; Iga, Mamoru; Rousseau, Jean Jacques
A Sociological and Statistical Study (Dublin), 49–51, 53–58
Sociological approach. See Society as locus of blame
Sociological method, 33
    See also Statistical approach
Socius, 8
Soma, 8
Spock, Benjamin, 89
Statistical approach, 33, 49, 104, 182
    See also Dublin, Louis I.; Durkheim, Emile

Stekel, Wilhelm, 91–92
Stoff, David M., 71–74, 75–85
Styron, William, 145
Subintentioned death, 92, 155
Substitutes for suicide, 18
Suggestion, 143
Suicidal ideation, 126, 144
Suicide: A Sociological and Statistical Study (Dublin), 49–51, 53–58
Suicide: A Study in Sociology (Durkheim), 33–35, 37–51
Suicide: Biopsychosocial Approaches (Botsis, ed.), 72
Suicide notes, 61, 124, 125
Suicide rest, 118
Suicide (Roy, ed.), 71–72
Suicides (Baechler), 103–122
"Suicide shrine," 190
    See also Popular locations
Suicidology, as term, 147
Survivors. *See* Significant others, impact on
Survivors of Suicide (Cain), 153–155, 157–165
Sussmilch, Johan, 33

Theories of suicide, 26, 61, 104
Third parties, 172
The Thorn in the Chrysanthemum: Suicide and Economic Success in Modern Japan (Iga), 59–61, 63–68
"To be or not to be," 14, 18, 22, 50
Tomita, Masako, 186
Transference, 169
Treatment, 77, 82–84, 136, 143, 183
    See also Medication; Postvention; Prevention; Psychotherapy
    Menninger and, 96
    neurobiology and, 76
Twentieth century, 26, 179–180, 182

Types of suicide
    for Baechler, 104–105, 106
    for Durkheim, 7, 34–35, 38
    for Menninger, 91, 92–93
    for Shneidman, 202–203

Ueki, Mieko, 186–187
Understanding, 9
Unhappiness, 29
United States
    American culture and, 60–61, 66–68
    Kennedy–Johnson–Nixon era in, 179–180
    war and suicide in, 56–57
Urban–rural differences, 54
The Use of Personal Documents in Psychological Science (Allport), 123–124

Value orientation, Japanese *vs.* American, 64, 65–68
Varah, Chad, 167–170, 171–177
Vengeance, 108
Vital psychological needs, 201

War, 54, 55–58
Warren, Harry, Jr., 195
Werther effect, 143
Widowhood, and suicide, 39, 43
Widows of suicide. *See* Significant others, impact on
Wish fulfillment, 142
Wittgenstein, Ludwig, 8
Wobber, H. B., 185, 188
Writers, suicides by, 24, 26, 61, 64, 66

Zeitgeist, 8–9, 90, 180
Zilboorg, Gregory, 8

ABOUT THE AUTHOR

Edwin S. Shneidman was born in York, Pennsylvania, in 1918. He grew up in Los Angeles and attended the University of California, Los Angeles (UCLA). He served in World War II, from the rank of private to captain. He received his PhD in 1948 from the University of Southern California under the G.I. Bill. He has held three main positions in his life. In the 1950s and 1960s, he was cofounder and codirector of the Los Angeles Suicide Prevention Center. From 1966 to 1969, he was chief of the Center for Studies of Suicide Prevention, National Institute of Mental Health (NIMH), Bethesda, Maryland. While at the NIMH he founded the American Association of Suicidology. From 1970 to 1988, he was professor of thanatology—first in the world—at his alma mater, UCLA. He is currently professor of thanatology emeritus.

In addition, he has been visiting professor at Harvard University and at the Ben Gurion University of the Negev, Israel; research associate at the Massachusetts General Hospital and the Karolinska Institute in Stockholm; and a Fellow at the Center for the Advanced Study of the Behavioral Sciences at Stanford University. He is a recipient of the Distinguished Professional Contributions to Public Service award from the American Psychological Association and of awards named for Bruno Klopfer, Harold M. Hildreth, Louis I. Dublin, and Henry A. Murray.

He has published 160 articles and chapters, edited 10 books on suicide and death, and authored *Deaths of Man*—nominated for a National Book Award; *Voices of Death*; *Definition of Suicide*; and *The Suicidal Mind*. Various books of his have been translated into French, German, Swedish, Russian, and Japanese.

He is married (since 1944) and has four children and six grandchildren.